I'm convinced that the Bible is somehow powerfully simple and beautifully complex. Like a diamond viewed from different angles, Scripture continually confronts my heart in fresh ways. This Bible-study series offers insightful perspectives and gives its participants a refreshing opportunity to admire the character of God and be transformed by the truth of his Word. Our souls need to meander through the minutiae and metanarrative of the Bible, and the **Storyline Bible Studies** help us do both.

KYLE IDLEMAN, senior pastor of Southeast Christian Church and bestselling author of *Not a Fan* and *One at a Time*

If you are longing for a breath of fresh air in your spiritual life, this study is for you. Kat Armstrong brings to life both familiar and less familiar Bible stories in such an engaging way that you can't help but see how the God of the past is also working and moving in your present. Through the captivating truths revealed in this series, you will discover more about God's faithfulness, be equipped to move past fear and disappointment, and be empowered to be who you were created to be. If your faith has felt mundane or routine, these words will be a refreshing balm to your soul and a guide to go deeper in your relationship with God.

HOSANNA WONG, international speaker and bestselling author of *How (Not) to Save the World: The Truth about Revealing God's Love to the People Right Next to You*

We are watching a new wave of Bible studies that care about the Bible's big story, from Genesis to Revelation; that plunge Bible readers into the depths of human despair and show them the glories of the Kingdom God plans for creation; and that invite readers to participate in that story in all its dimensions—in the mountains and the valleys. Anyone who ponders these Bible studies will come to terms not only with the storyline of the Bible but also with where each of us fits in God's grand narrative. I heartily commend Kat's **Storyline Bible Studies**.

REV. CANON DR. SCOT McKNIGHT, New Testament scholar, author, professor, and host of the *Kingdom Roots* podcast

Kat Armstrong is an able trail guide with contagious enthusiasm! In this series, she'll take you hiking through Scripture to experience mountains and valleys, sticks and stones, sinners and saints. If you are relatively new to the Bible or are struggling to see how it all fits together, your trek with Kat will be well worth it. You might even decide that hiking through the Bible is your new hobby.

CARMEN JOY IMES, associate professor of Old Testament at Biola University and author of *Bearing God's Name: Why Sinai Still Matters*

Kat Armstrong takes you into the heart of Scripture so that Scripture can grow in your heart. The **Storyline Bible Studies** have everything: the overarching story of God's redemption, the individual biblical story's historical context, and the text's interpretation that connects with today's realities. Armstrong asks insightful questions that make the Bible come alive and draws authentically on her own faith journey so that readers might deepen their relationship with Jesus. Beautifully written and accessible, the **Storyline Bible Studies** are a wonderful resource for individual or group study.

LYNN H. COHICK, PhD, distinguished professor of New Testament and director of Houston Theological Seminary at Houston Christian University

Christians affirm that the Bible is God's Word and provides God's life-giving instruction and encouragement. But what good is such an authoritative and valuable text if God's people don't engage it to find the help the Scriptures provide? Here's where Kat Armstrong's studies shine. In each volume, she presents Bible study as a journey through Scripture that can be transformational. In the process, she enables readers to see the overarching storyline of the Bible and to find their place in that story. In addition, Armstrong reinforces the essential steps that make Bible study life-giving for people seeking to grow in their faith. Whether for individuals, for small groups, or as part of a church curriculum, these studies are ideally suited to draw students into a fresh and invigorating engagement with God's Word.

WILLIAM W. KLEIN, PhD, professor emeritus of New Testament interpretation and author of *Handbook for Personal Bible Study: Enriching Your Experience with God's Word*

Kat has done two things that I love. She's taken something that is familiar and presented it in a fresh way that is understandable by all, balancing the profound with accessibility. And her trustworthy and constant approach to Bible study equips the participant to emerge from this study with the ability to keep studying and growing more.

MARTY SOLOMON, creator and executive producer of *The BEMA Podcast*

You are in for an adventure. In this series, Kat pulls back the curtain to reveal how intentionally God has woven together seemingly disconnected moments in the collective Bible story. Her delivery is both brilliant and approachable. She will invite you to be a curious sleuth as you navigate familiar passages of Scripture, discovering things you'd never seen before. I promise you will never read the living Word the same again.

JENN JETT BARRETT, founder and visionary of The Well Summit

Kat has done it again! The same wisdom, depth, humility, and authenticity that we have come to expect from her previous work is on full display here in her new **Storyline Bible Study** series. Kat is the perfect guide through these important themes and through the story of Scripture: gentle and generous on the one hand, capable and clear on the other. She is a gifted communicator and teacher of God's Word. The format of these studies is helpful too—perfect pacing, just the right amount of new information at each turn, with plenty of space for writing and prayerful reflection as you go and some great resources for further study. I love learning from Kat, and I'm sure you will too. Grab a few friends from your church or neighborhood and dig into these incredible resources together to find your imagination awakened and your faith strengthened.

DAN LOWERY, president of Pillar Seminary

Kat Armstrong possesses something I deeply admire: a sincere and abiding respect for the Bible. Her tenaciousness to know more about her beloved Christ, her commitment to truth telling, and her desire to dig until she mines the deepest gold for her Bible-study readers makes her one of my favorite Bible teachers. I find few that match her scriptural attentiveness and even fewer that embody her humble spirit. This project is stunning, like the rest of her work.

LISA WHITTLE, bestselling author of *Jesus over Everything: Uncomplicating the Daily Struggle to Put Jesus First*, Bible teacher, and podcast host

GARDENS

GROWING AN EVERGREEN FAITH
IN A TRUSTWORTHY GOD

KAT ARMSTRONG

Published in alliance with Tyndale House Publishers

NavPress.com

Gardens: Growing an Evergreen Faith in a Trustworthy God

A NavPress resource published in alliance with Tyndale House Publishers

The Team:
David Zimmerman, Publisher; Caitlyn Carlson, Acquisitions Editor; Elizabeth Schroll, Copyeditor; Lacie Phillips, Production Assistant; Lindsey Bergsma, Designer; Sarah Ocenasek, Proofreading Coordinator

For information about special discounts for bulk purchases, please contact Tyndale House Publishers at csresponse@tyndale.com, or call 1-855-277-9400.

ISBN 978-1-64158-887-4

Printed in the United States of America

31 30 29 28 27 26 25
7 6 5 4 3 2 1

For my dad, Ronald K. Obenhaus.

I think you would have loved this.

Contents

A Message from Kat

I HAVE NO BUSINESS writing about gardens. I can't keep any plants alive, and honestly, I don't care to try. I'm fine living in a concrete jungle and buying my produce from the grocery store. The only thing that could interest me in a gardening hobby would be a guaranteed best friendship with Joanna Gaines—who, according to her shows and magazines, really loves spending time in her garden, watching things grow.

Gardens in the Bible, however, occupy a lot of my brain space. After all, God bookends his Word with stories about celestial gardens. The Bible begins with a story about God planting a garden in Eden and ends with a story about God replanting Christians in a Garden City called the new Jerusalem.

I find myself desperately fixated on that final Garden City, where the apostle John says death and tears are gone (Revelation 21:4) and only life and light remain. I need the new Jerusalem to be real. I've had enough of death and pain and weariness. I cling to the promise of always-and-forever abundant, endless life.

As I began my research on gardens in the Bible, I wanted more out of my relationship with Christ. I've experienced the "abundant life" at times. But somewhere along the way, I grew distracted, stressed, and tired.

Do you find yourself longing for a spiritual life that is abundant—where you are not just scraping by but enduring and flourishing?

In all the past seasons of life when I experienced immense growth in my faith, I was absorbing every last nutrient from the soil of Scripture. I was soaking in the sunlight of Bible verses illuminated and drinking in God's Living Water, his Spirit. I want that again. I want my faith to spring up—to be vibrant, not static. To have deep, sturdy roots, not feel flimsy or droopy.

Here's what I know for sure: Every garden in Scripture is a landmark for my faith—and for yours. The *Gardens* Bible study is an invitation to explore God's literary genius and masterful storytelling, to approach the themes and threads of his Word with curiosity and hope. As we follow the garden theme from Genesis to Revelation, I can promise you this: We'll find Christ's presence in all the gardens we're exploring, inviting us into an evergreen faith.

Love,

Kat

The Lord will guide you continually,
and satisfy your needs in parched places,
and make your bones strong;
and you shall be like a watered garden,
like a spring of water,
whose waters never fail.

ISAIAH 58:11

The Storyline of Scripture

YOUR DECISION TO STUDY THE BIBLE for the next few weeks is no accident—God has brought you here, to this moment. And I don't want to take it for granted. Here, at the beginning, I want to invite you into the most important step you can take, the one that brings the whole of the Bible alive in extraordinary ways: a relationship with Jesus.

The Bible is a collection of divinely inspired manuscripts written over fifteen hundred years by at least forty different authors. Together, the manuscripts make up tens of thousands of verses, sixty-six books, and two testaments. Point being: It's a lot of content.

But the Bible is really just one big story: God's story of redemption. From Genesis to Revelation the Bible includes narratives, songs, poems, wisdom literature, letters, and even apocalyptic prophecies. Yet everything we read in God's Word helps us understand God's love and his plan to be in a relationship with us.

If you hear nothing else, hear this: God loves you.

It's easy to get lost in the vast amount of information in the Bible, so we're going to explore the storyline of Scripture in four parts. And as you locate your experience in the story of the Bible, I hope the story of redemption becomes your own.

PART 1: GOD MADE SOMETHING GOOD.

The big story—God's story of redemption—started in a garden. When God launched his project for humanity, he purposed all of us—his image bearers—to flourish and co-create with him. In the beginning there was peace, beauty, order, and abundant life. The soil was good. Life was good. We rarely hear this part of our story, but it doesn't make it less true. God created something good—and that includes you.

PART 2: WE MESSED IT UP.

If you've ever thought, *This isn't how it's supposed to be*, you're right. It's not. We messed up God's good world. Do you ever feel like you've won gold medals in messing things up? Me too. All humanity shares in that brokenness. We are imperfect. The people we love are imperfect. Our systems are jacked, and our world is broken. And that's on us. We made the mess, and we literally can't help ourselves. We need to be rescued from our circumstances, the systems in which we live, and ourselves.

PART 3: JESUS MAKES IT RIGHT.

The good news is that God can clean up all our messes, and he does so through the life, death, and resurrection of Jesus Christ. No one denies that Jesus lived and died. That's just history. It's the empty tomb and the hundreds of eyewitnesses who saw Jesus after his death that make us scratch our heads. Because science can only prove something that is repeatable, we are dependent upon the eyewitness testimonies of Jesus' resurrection for this once-in-history moment. If Jesus rose from the dead—and I believe he did—Jesus is exactly who he said he was, and he accomplished exactly what had been predicted for thousands of years. He restored us. Jesus made *it*, all of it, right. He can forgive your sins and connect you to the holy God through his life, death, and resurrection.

PART 4: ONE DAY, GOD WILL MAKE ALL THINGS NEW.

The best news is that this is not as good as it gets. A day is coming when Christ will return. He's coming back to re-create our world: a place with no tears, no pain, no suffering, no brokenness, no helplessness—just love. God will make all things new. In the meantime, God invites you to step into his storyline, to join him in his work of restoring all things. Rescued restorers live with purpose and on mission: not a life devoid of hardship, but one filled with enduring hope.

RESPONDING TO GOD'S STORYLINE

If the storyline of Scripture feels like a lightbulb turning on in your soul, that, my friend, is the one true, living God, who eternally exists as Father, Son, and Holy Spirit. God is inviting you into a relationship with him to have your sins forgiven and secure a place in his presence forever. When you locate your story within God's story of redemption, you begin a lifelong relationship with God that brings meaning, hope, and restoration to your life.

Take a moment now to begin a relationship with Christ:

God, I believe the story of the Bible, that Jesus is Lord and you raised him from the dead to forgive my sins and make our relationship possible. Your storyline is now my story. I want to learn how to love you and share your love with others. Amen.

If you confess with your lips that Jesus is Lord and believe in your heart that God raised him from the dead, you will be saved.

ROMANS 10:9

How to Use This Bible Study

THE **STORYLINE BIBLE STUDIES** are versatile and can be used for

- individual study (self-paced),
- small groups (five- or ten-lesson curriculum), or
- church ministry (semester-long curriculum).

INDIVIDUAL STUDY

Each lesson in the *Gardens* Bible study is divided into four fifteen- to twenty-minute parts (sixty to eighty minutes of individual study time per lesson). You can work through the material one part at a time over a few different days or all in one sitting. Either way, this study will be like anything good in your life: What you put in, you get out. Each of the four parts of each lesson will help you practice Bible-study methods.

SMALL GROUPS

Working through the *Gardens* Bible study with a group could be a catalyst for life change. Although the Holy Spirit can teach you truth when you read the Bible on your own, I want to encourage you to gather a small group together to work through this study for these reasons:

- God himself is in communion as one essence and three persons: Father, Son, and Holy Spirit.
- Interconnected, interdependent relationships are hallmarks of the Christian faith life.
- When we collaborate with each other in Bible study, we have access to the viewpoints of our brothers and sisters in Christ, which enrich our understanding of the truth.

For this Bible study, every small-group member will need a copy of the *Gardens* study guide. In addition, I've created a free downloadable small-group guide that includes

- discussion questions for each lesson,
- Scripture readings, and
- prayer prompts.

Whether you've been a discussion leader for decades or just volunteered to lead a group for the first time, you'll find the resources you need to create a loving atmosphere for men and women to grow in Christlikeness. You can download the small-group guide using this QR code.

CHURCH MINISTRY

Church and ministry leaders: Your work is sacred. I know that planning and leading through a semester of ministry can be both challenging and rewarding. That's why every **Storyline Bible Study** is written so that you can build modular semesters of ministry. The *Gardens* Bible study is designed to complement the

Deserts Bible study. Together, *Gardens* and *Deserts* can support a whole semester of ministry seamlessly, inviting the people you lead into God's Word and making your life simpler.

To further equip church and ministry leaders, I've created *The Leader's Guide*, a free digital resource. You can download *The Leader's Guide* using this QR code.

The Leader's Guide offers these resources:

- a sample ministry calendar for a ten-plus-lesson semester of ministry,
- small-group discussion questions for each lesson,
- Scripture readings for each lesson,
- prayer prompts for each lesson,
- five teaching topics for messages that could be taught in large-group settings, and
- resources for deeper study.

SPECIAL FEATURES

However you decide to utilize the *Gardens* Bible study, whether for individual, self-paced devotional time; as a small-group curriculum; or for semester-long church ministry, you'll notice several stand-out features unique to the **Storyline Bible Studies**:

- gospel presentation at the beginning of each Bible study;
- full Scripture passages included in the study so that you can mark up the text and keep your notes in one place;
- insights from diverse scholars, authors, and Bible teachers;
- an emphasis on close readings of large portions of Scripture;
- following one theme instead of focusing on one verse or passage;
- Christological narrative theology without a lot of church-y words; and
- retrospective or imaginative readings of the Bible to help Christians follow the storyline of Scripture.

You may have studied the Bible by book, topic, or passage before; all those approaches are enriching ways to read the Word of God. The **Storyline Bible Studies** follow a literary thread to deepen your appreciation for God's master plan of redemption and develop your skill in connecting the Old Testament to the New.

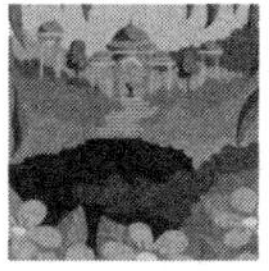

INTRODUCTION

THE GARDENS STORYLINE

GOD'S GOT A GREEN THUMB. He is the ultimate Gardener, specializing in planting seeds of faith and providing nutrient-rich soil for our faith to grow. And only our expert Gardener can somehow, miraculously, bring dead, fruitless plants back to life, where they not only grow but bear *much* fruit. If there's anyone we need guiding us toward the abundant life, it's him. He knows how to cultivate.

The Bible is a literary masterpiece for infinite reasons, and one way God's artistic brilliance unfolds is through his storied settings—the geographical locations of the stories he has preserved for us in Scripture. As you may have seen through other **Storyline Bible Studies**, places didn't just matter in the ancient world—they had meaning. Locations are not solely pins on a map; they are loaded with historical significance and serve as connection points unifying God's story of redemption from the Old Testament to the New.

The God who planted a garden in Eden, placing Adam and Eve in it to cultivate all God's creation, is the same God who suffered the agony of abandonment and self-sacrifice in the Garden of Gethsemane, who revealed himself to the first gospel preacher at the Gardens of the Crucifixion and Resurrection, and who is the King of the new Garden City in Revelation.

As we zero in on the different gardens in Scripture, you and I are going to discover this all-important truth: God is sacrificially committed to our flourishing. He doesn't expect us to just spontaneously start growing in love, joy, peace, patience, kindness, goodness, faithfulness, gentleness, and self-control. He's the Vine. He's producing the fruit of his Holy Spirit in our lives. Our responsibility is to remain connected to him and to trust that his boundaries are what cultivate goodness and abundance in our lives.

The *Gardens* Bible study will guide you through five Bible stories set in gardens. The presence of these places in the Scriptures is a key element in each story, revealing something about God—and about us. As we begin in the paradise of Eden and move through other gardens in Scripture, we will be on a journey to find the paradise that's been lost. The good news is that the good Gardener can be trusted to plant *and* replant us in the story of redemption.

In the *Gardens* Bible study, we're going to explore

- *Genesis 1–3*: the Garden of Eden, where the first humans made a choice between trusting God and trusting themselves;
- *Esther 1, 7*: the Garden of Ahasuerus, where human dysfunction creates an antigarden motif;
- *Matthew 26*: the Garden of Gethsemane, where Jesus wrestled with the sacrifice before him;
- *John 19–20*: the Gardens of the Crucifixion and Resurrection, where the resurrected Jesus revealed himself to Mary Magdalene; and
- *Revelation 21–22*: the Garden City, where God will replant Christians in the new Jerusalem.

We're going to do this by looking at each garden story through four different lenses:

- **PART 1: CONTEXT.** Do you ever feel dropped into a Bible story disoriented? Part 1 will introduce you to the garden you're going to study and help you study its story in its scriptural context. Getting your bearings before you read will enable you to answer the question *What am I about to read?*
- **PART 2: SEEING.** Do you ever read on autopilot? I do too. Sometimes I finish reading without a clue as to what just happened. A better way to read the Bible is to practice thoughtful, close reading of Scripture to absorb the message God is offering to us. That's why part 2 includes close Scripture reading and observation questions to empower you to answer the question *What is the story saying?*
- **PART 3: UNDERSTANDING.** If you've ever scratched your head after reading your Bible, part 3 will give you the tools to understand the author's intended meaning both for the original audience and for you. Plus you'll practice connecting the Old and New Testaments to get a fuller picture of God's unchanging grace. Part 3 will enable you to answer the question *What does it mean?*
- **PART 4: RESPONDING.** The purpose of Bible study is to help you become more Christlike; that's why part 4 will include journaling space for your reflection on and responses to the content and a blank checklist for actionable next steps. You'll be able to process what you're learning so that you can live out the concepts and pursue Christlikeness. Part 4 will enable you to answer the questions *What truths is this passage teaching?* and *How do I apply this to my life?*

One of my prayers for you, as a curious Bible reader, is that our journey through this study will help you cultivate a biblical imagination so that you're able to make connections throughout the whole storyline of the Bible. In each lesson, I'll do my best to include a few verses from different places in the Bible that are connected to our garden stories. In the course of this study, we'll see the way God shows up in gardens throughout his Word—and get a glimpse of how he might show up in our lives today.

God's Word is so wonderful, I hardly know how to contain my excitement. Feel free to geek out with me; let your geek flag fly high, my friends. When we can see how interrelated all the parts of Scripture are to each other, we'll find our affection for God stirred as we see his artistic brilliance unfold.

LESSON ONE

TRUSTING GOD'S BOUNDARIES

THE GARDEN OF EDEN:
A FOOL'S PARADISE

SCRIPTURE: GENESIS 1–3

PART 1

CONTEXT

Before you begin your study, we will start with the context of the story we are about to read together: the setting, both cultural and historical; the people involved; and where our passage fits in the larger setting of Scripture. All these things help us make sense of what we're reading. Understanding the context of a Bible story is fundamental to reading Scripture well. Getting your bearings before you read will enable you to answer the question *What am I about to read?*

GARDENERS TAKE GREAT PRIDE in their produce. My uncle Rod loves to brag that his Austin-grown lettuce is better than any other greens around. My friend Chris enjoys measuring the various sizes of his watermelons. And I can personally attest that my friend Jamie's chocolate-mint herb is delicious. Intentional gardeners celebrate and share the fruits of their labor.

That's what God did with his garden project in Eden too. He intentionally planted a garden and then celebrated what he'd cultivated. At the end of each day of Creation, God surveyed his work and declared it good. The waters under the sky were good. The dry land was good. All the vegetation, the plants and the grass and the fruit trees, were good too. The lights in the sky were good. All the living creatures swimming in the waters, flying in the sky, or moving on land—they were good, good, good.

You know what God called *very* good? Adam and Eve. They were more than just good—because they were made in God's image. Together they were meant to reflect God's glory, to be his vice-regents on earth, and to care for and cultivate everything God had created. They were supposed to be good gardeners like the good Gardener.

The problem is, instead of living up to their cultural mandate, Adam and Eve decided to pursue wisdom apart from God. And the garden project they were supposed to cultivate failed epically. Everyone and everything suffered because Adam and Eve refused to listen to God's wisdom. Instead, they chose to take matters into their own hands.

We see Adam and Eve's story repeated again and again throughout human history. The Garden of Eden is more than a historical location; it shows us the patterns of our lives and the state of the human soul.

But this garden was also where God planted the first seeds of our redemption, amid trees and flowers—a place called Eden, the name of which is sometimes translated from Hebrew as *joy*, *finery*, or *delight*.[1] Our journey begins in God's delight, his paradise, our paradise—and one day, God's saving grace will lead us somewhere even better than Eden.

Without some context, we may be tempted to read Genesis as a stand-alone book of the Bible. But Genesis is not a stand-alone book; it is one part of a five-part literary unit called the Pentateuch. Or put another way: The Pentateuch is a single body of literature with five unique but cohesive parts. The writer of the Pentateuch, Moses, wanted us to—and assumed we would—read all five parts as a unit. Additionally, Moses would have assumed that his audience understood why he was writing Genesis, why the garden in Eden mattered, and to whom it would matter.

Moses was likely writing what became the book of Genesis during the Israelites' exodus from Egypt and leading up to the conquest of the Promised Land—which meant he was writing to people who had experienced God's liberating power from evil forces, the refining wanderings and miraculous provision in the wilderness, and the giving of the law. God's people were standing at the precipice of finally entering his Promised Land.

God's people were people of promise, but the promise hadn't come to pass yet. So they were having an identity crisis. Would they be garden dwellers again, or would they live forever exiled in the wilderness? Would they finally reach the Promised Land, or would they die in the desert? In a very real sense, this generation—who lived in the wilderness because their parents had repeated Adam and Eve's rejection of God's wisdom—must have been questioning God's trustworthiness. And wondering if God was holding out on them.

Moses needed his people to remember the past so they could face their future. God's people needed to be reminded why they'd been created: that their purpose was to bless all nations. They needed to be reminded of their identity: that they were loved and chosen by God to bring his love to all the world. And they needed to understand their relationship with God: that they were covenant members of God's community, beloved and fought for by a faithful God powerful enough to overthrow Pharaoh.

> Genesis introduces us to an awesome God who holds a good world in loving hands.[2]
>
> Rodney S. Sadler Jr., "Genesis," in *The Africana Bible*

You and I are invited into the same lesson, the same clarification of our identity. Are we going to live this life as garden dwellers, with all the resources God intends for our flourishing? Will we trust God enough to appreciate, honor, and respect the boundaries he sets for us? Or will we continue, through our own sinful actions, to reject God's wisdom and get expelled from paradise? Will we be paradise-lost people or people-who-walk-with-God-in-his-garden people?

The story set in the Garden of Eden shows us that God can be trusted. And it will help us trust God more. Trust the good Gardener's cultivation skills. And enjoy the way God celebrates the work of his hands. The way God celebrates us, the apple of his eye.

1. **PERSONAL CONTEXT: What is going on in your life right now that might impact how you understand the Garden of Eden story? What do you hope to learn from this lesson?**

2. **SPIRITUAL CONTEXT: If you've never studied the Garden of Eden before, what piques your curiosity? If you've studied this place before, what impressions and insights do you recall?**

3. **BIBLICAL CONTEXT: What questions come to mind as you read about the context of Genesis, the Garden of Eden, and the Israelites' history? What questions do you wish you could have answered before studying this part of Scripture?**

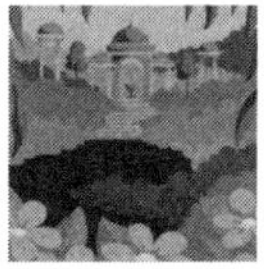

PART 2

SEEING

Seeing the text is vital if we want the heart of the Scripture passage to sink in. We read slowly and intentionally through the text with the context in mind. As we practice close, thoughtful reading of Scripture, we pick up on phrases, implications, and meanings we might otherwise have missed. Part 2 includes close Scripture reading and observation questions to empower you to answer the question *What is the story saying?*

1. **Read Genesis 1. As you go along, label and draw brackets alongside the portions that cover these four topics: *time*, *weather*, *food*, and *people*.**

1 In the beginning when God created the heavens and the earth, [2] the
earth was a formless void and darkness covered the face of the deep,
while a wind from God swept over the face of the waters. [3] Then God said,
"Let there be light"; and there was light. [4] And God saw that the light was
good; and God separated the light from the darkness. [5] God called the
light Day, and the darkness he called Night. And there was evening and
there was morning, the first day.

[6] And God said, "Let there be a dome in the midst of the waters, and
let it separate the waters from the waters." [7] So God made the dome and
separated the waters that were under the dome from the waters that

were above the dome. And it was so. 8 God called the dome Sky. And there
was evening and there was morning, the second day.

9 And God said, "Let the waters under the sky be gathered together
into one place, and let the dry land appear." And it was so. 10 God called
the dry land Earth, and the waters that were gathered together he called
Seas. And God saw that it was good. 11 Then God said, "Let the earth
put forth vegetation: plants yielding seed, and fruit trees of every kind
on earth that bear fruit with the seed in it." And it was so. 12 The earth
brought forth vegetation: plants yielding seed of every kind, and trees of
every kind bearing fruit with the seed in it. And God saw that it was good.
13 And there was evening and there was morning, the third day.

14 And God said, "Let there be lights in the dome of the sky to separate
the day from the night; and let them be for signs and for seasons and for
days and years, 15 and let them be lights in the dome of the sky to give
light upon the earth." And it was so. 16 God made the two great lights—the
greater light to rule the day and the lesser light to rule the night—and the
stars. 17 God set them in the dome of the sky to give light upon the earth,
18 to rule over the day and over the night, and to separate the light from
the darkness. And God saw that it was good. 19 And there was evening
and there was morning, the fourth day.

20 And God said, "Let the waters bring forth swarms of living creatures,
and let birds fly above the earth across the dome of the sky." 21 So God
created the great sea monsters and every living creature that moves, of
every kind, with which the waters swarm, and every winged bird of every
kind. And God saw that it was good. 22 God blessed them, saying, "Be
fruitful and multiply and fill the waters in the seas, and let birds multiply on
the earth." 23 And there was evening and there was morning, the fifth day.

24 And God said, "Let the earth bring forth living creatures of every kind:
cattle and creeping things and wild animals of the earth of every kind." And
it was so. 25 God made the wild animals of the earth of every kind, and the
cattle of every kind, and everything that creeps upon the ground of every
kind. And God saw that it was good.

26 Then God said, "Let us make humankind in our image, according to
our likeness; and let them have dominion over the fish of the sea, and over
the birds of the air, and over the cattle, and over all the wild animals of the
earth, and over every creeping thing that creeps upon the earth."

27 So God created humankind in his image,
in the image of God he created them;
male and female he created them.

28 God blessed them, and God said to them, "Be fruitful and multiply, and
fill the earth and subdue it; and have dominion over the fish of the sea and
over the birds of the air and over every living thing that moves upon the
earth." 29 God said, "See, I have given you every plant yielding seed that is
upon the face of all the earth, and every tree with seed in its fruit; you shall
have them for food. 30 And to every beast of the earth, and to every bird of
the air, and to everything that creeps on the earth, everything that has the
breath of life, I have given every green plant for food." And it was so. 31 God
saw everything that he had made, and indeed, it was very good. And there
was evening and there was morning, the sixth day.

GENESIS 1

2. What do you learn about God from Genesis 1:26?

Moses, writing under the inspiration of the Holy Spirit, reveals God's conversation with himself before time began. The one true, triune God eternally exists in three persons—Father, Son, and Holy Spirit—and his first conversation recorded in Scripture is in collaboration and community with himself. The man and woman, created as God's image bearers, reflect God's unity and diversity, his oneness and distinction.

3. Using Genesis 1:28, list the things God blesses human beings—male and female—to do on earth.

Both the man and the woman are given these blessed tasks. Both are deputized as God's working agents on earth. Both are needed. Both are important.

If you'd asked me twenty years ago about the division of labor in the Garden of Eden, I would have gendered God's blessings. Somewhere along the way, I started to believe that the first man, and therefore all men, was supposed to rule. And the first woman, and therefore all women, was created to multiply. Maybe it was my failure to read carefully. Or misguided messages I received in church or church culture. Whatever the case, I thought ruling and subduing were tasks for men and being fruitful and multiplying were tasks for women. But Scripture says otherwise.

4. Which aspects of creation are the man and the woman commanded to rule together? (Leave the box unchecked if it is something only one person is to do.)

- ☐ rule the fish of the sea
- ☐ rule the birds of the air
- ☐ rule the cattle
- ☐ rule the whole earth and the creatures that live on the earth

God seems to emphasize this point. The woman and the man need each other; they are to work together to rule everything. Underneath it all—literally underneath the fish, birds, livestock, and other creatures—is the land, the earth itself. As much as the first chapter of the Bible is about introducing us to some main characters of the story, it is also introducing us to our main setting: a garden. This land, protected by God, planted by God, foreshadows the later gift of the Promised Land.

Genesis 1 is the first of two stories of God's Creation; the second story immediately follows it in Genesis 2. You'll notice that while the first story outlines the origin and process of Creation, this second one gets more into the details of the creation of the man and woman, and we learn their names for the first time: Adam and Eve.

5. Read Genesis 2 and underline any details concerning the Garden of Eden.

2 Thus the heavens and the earth were finished, and all their multitude.
2 And on the seventh day God finished the work that he had done, and he
rested on the seventh day from all the work that he had done. 3 So God
blessed the seventh day and hallowed it, because on it God rested from all
the work that he had done in creation.

4 These are the generations of the heavens and the earth when they
were created.

In the day that the LORD God made the earth and the heavens,
5 when no plant of the field was yet in the earth and no herb of the field
had yet sprung up—for the LORD God had not caused it to rain upon the
earth, and there was no one to till the ground; 6 but a stream would rise
from the earth, and water the whole face of the ground—7 then the LORD
God formed man from the dust of the ground, and breathed into his
nostrils the breath of life; and the man became a living being. 8 And the
LORD God planted a garden in Eden, in the east; and there he put the
man whom he had formed. 9 Out of the ground the LORD God made to
grow every tree that is pleasant to the sight and good for food, the tree

of life also in the midst of the garden, and the tree of the knowledge of
good and evil.

10 A river flows out of Eden to water the garden, and from there it
divides and becomes four branches. 11 The name of the first is Pishon; it is
the one that flows around the whole land of Havilah, where there is gold;
12 and the gold of that land is good; bdellium and onyx stone are there.
13 The name of the second river is Gihon; it is the one that flows around the
whole land of Cush. 14 The name of the third river is Tigris, which flows east
of Assyria. And the fourth river is the Euphrates.

15 The LORD God took the man and put him in the garden of Eden to
till it and keep it. 16 And the LORD God commanded the man, "You may
freely eat of every tree of the garden; 17 but of the tree of the knowledge
of good and evil you shall not eat, for in the day that you eat of it you
shall die."

18 Then the LORD God said, "It is not good that the man should be
alone; I will make him a helper as his partner." 19 So out of the ground the
LORD God formed every animal of the field and every bird of the air, and
brought them to the man to see what he would call them; and whatever
the man called every living creature, that was its name. 20 The man gave
names to all cattle, and to the birds of the air, and to every animal of the
field; but for the man there was not found a helper as his partner. 21 So
the LORD God caused a deep sleep to fall upon the man, and he slept; then
he took one of his ribs and closed up its place with flesh. 22 And the rib
that the LORD God had taken from the man he made into a woman and
brought her to the man. 23 Then the man said,

"This at last is bone of my bones
    and flesh of my flesh;
this one shall be called Woman,
    for out of Man this one was taken."

[24] Therefore a man leaves his father and his mother and clings to his wife, and they become one flesh. [25] And the man and his wife were both naked, and were not ashamed.

GENESIS 2

6. Using the details you underlined, pretend you are a modern-day real estate agent, and write out a website listing for this plot of land.

One of my best friends, Sarah Conner, wrote a hilarious answer to this prompt. Using the voice and cadence of Stefon, a *Saturday Night Live* sketch character, she started her description with "This garden has *everything* . . ."

Here's my answer: beautiful trees, tasty fruit, pure gold, and well-watered land. These are key selling points of the Garden of Eden. Moses takes his time to give us lots of details about God's garden project. It had everything one could need.

7. What does God say is "not good" in the Garden of Eden?

Adam without Eve is a problem. The first chapter of Genesis has already told us why: Adam and Eve are equally called, equally responsible, to work together.

> The man does not name the woman in Genesis 2; he calls her what she is. The passive construction, "she shall be called Woman," does not indicate that he gave her a name. Further, "woman" (*ishah*) is not her name. He is man (*ish*) and she is woman (*ishah*). What they share in common is their "*ish*-ness"—they are both human. But they are not the same; he is male and she is female. And that is the narrator's point, that there is unity and diversity; they are one but different. They are equal, but not the same.[3]
>
> **Glenn Kreider, "Eve," in *Vindicating the Vixens***

The word translated "helper" (Hebrew *ʿēzer*) shows up twenty-one times in the Old Testament. And if you study carefully all the uses of this word, you'll be able to discern what meaning Moses intends in Genesis 2:18. It is not a diminished or secondary role. Eve was Adam's worthy complement, a capable counterpart prepared to face every challenge alongside Adam. And she would double the impact of their work.

HELPER OR *ʿĒZER* IN THE OLD TESTAMENT

Verse in which *ʿēzer* is mentioned	Who is the helper in this verse?	How is the helper supposed to help in this verse?
Genesis 2:18	Eve	Eve becomes the counterpart to Adam.
Genesis 2:20	Eve	Eve becomes the counterpart to Adam.
Exodus 18:4	God	God delivers Israel from the sword of Pharaoh.
Deuteronomy 33:7	God	Moses asks God to deliver Judah by fighting against their adversaries.
Deuteronomy 33:26	God	God rides through the heavens to deliver his people.
Deuteronomy 33:29	God	God shields his people from their enemies, making the enemies come fawning to them.

Verse in which ʿēzer is mentioned	Who is the helper in this verse?	How is the helper supposed to help in this verse?
Psalm 20:2	God	God is asked to send help from his sanctuary.
Psalm 33:20	God	God shields the people who wait for him.
Psalm 70:5	God	God is asked to deliver the psalmist when he is poor and needy.
Psalm 89:19	God	God gives help to his chosen king.
Psalm 115:9	God	God, the shield of Israel, is worthy of trust.
Psalm 115:10	God	God, the shield of Aaron, is worthy of trust.
Psalm 115:11	God	God, the shield of all who fear him, is worthy of trust.
Psalm 121:1	God	God is the helper of those who look to him.
Psalm 121:2	God	God is the helper capable even of creating heaven and earth.
Psalm 124:8	God	God is the helper capable even of creating heaven and earth.
Psalm 146:5	God	The God of Jacob is the helper of his people.
Isaiah 30:5	non-Israelite nations	The non-Israelite nations fail to provide the nation of Israel with military aid.
Ezekiel 12:14	non-Israelite nations	The non-Israelite nations provide the nation of Israel with military aid.
Daniel 11:34	freedom fighters	Israel receives help throwing off a foreign oppressor.
Hosea 13:9	God	God is the only One who can help Israel, who is facing destruction.

8. How many times is ʿ*ēzer* used to refer to God? ______

To Eve? ______

To warriors? ______

9. **Based on the uses of *helper* (*ʿēzer*) in the Old Testament, how does God help his people?**

10. **Based on the uses of *helper* (*ʿēzer*) in the Old Testament, what kind of help do you think Eve was created to offer Adam?**

11. **Read Genesis 3. Underline anything that changes for the serpent, Adam, Eve, or the Garden of Eden.**

3 Now the serpent was more crafty than any other wild animal that the
LORD God had made. He said to the woman, "Did God say, 'You shall not
eat from any tree in the garden'?" 2 The woman said to the serpent, "We
may eat of the fruit of the trees in the garden; 3 but God said, 'You shall not
eat of the fruit of the tree that is in the middle of the garden, nor shall you
touch it, or you shall die.'" 4 But the serpent said to the woman, "You will
not die; 5 for God knows that when you eat of it your eyes will be opened,
and you will be like God, knowing good and evil." 6 So when the woman saw

that the tree was good for food, and that it was a delight to the eyes, and
that the tree was to be desired to make one wise, she took of its fruit and
ate; and she also gave some to her husband, who was with her, and he ate.
[7] Then the eyes of both were opened, and they knew that they were naked;
and they sewed fig leaves together and made loincloths for themselves.

[8] They heard the sound of the LORD God walking in the garden at the
time of the evening breeze, and the man and his wife hid themselves from
the presence of the LORD God among the trees of the garden. [9] But the
LORD God called to the man, and said to him, "Where are you?" [10] He said,
"I heard the sound of you in the garden, and I was afraid, because I was
naked; and I hid myself." [11] He said, "Who told you that you were naked?
Have you eaten from the tree of which I commanded you not to eat?"
[12] The man said, "The woman whom you gave to be with me, she gave me
fruit from the tree, and I ate." [13] Then the LORD God said to the woman,
"What is this that you have done?" The woman said, "The serpent tricked
me, and I ate." [14] The LORD God said to the serpent,

"Because you have done this,
    cursed are you among all animals
    and among all wild creatures;
upon your belly you shall go,
    and dust you shall eat
    all the days of your life.
[15] I will put enmity between you and the woman,
    and between your offspring and hers;
he will strike your head,
    and you will strike his heel."

[16] To the woman he said,

"I will greatly increase your pangs in childbearing;
    in pain you shall bring forth children,

yet your desire shall be for your husband,
and he shall rule over you."

[17] And to the man he said,

"Because you have listened to the voice of your wife,
and have eaten of the tree
about which I commanded you,
'You shall not eat of it,'
cursed is the ground because of you;
in toil you shall eat of it all the days of your life;
[18] thorns and thistles it shall bring forth for you;
and you shall eat the plants of the field.
[19] By the sweat of your face
you shall eat bread
until you return to the ground,
for out of it you were taken;
you are dust,
and to dust you shall return."

[20] The man named his wife Eve, because she was the mother of all
living. [21] And the LORD God made garments of skins for the man and his
wife, and clothed them.

[22] Then the LORD God said, "See, the man has become like one of us,
knowing good and evil; and now, he might reach out his hand and take
also from the tree of life, and eat, and live forever"–[23]therefore the LORD
God sent him forth from the garden of Eden, to till the ground from which
he was taken. [24] He drove out the man; and at the east of the garden of
Eden he placed the cherubim, and a sword flaming and turning to guard
the way to the tree of life.

GENESIS 3

12. Describe the before and after of . . .

- **the serpent**

- **the woman**

- **the man**

- **the land**

Do you notice the difference between how God talked to the man and the woman and how he condemned the serpent and the land? Adam wasn't cursed. Eve wasn't cursed. The serpent and the land were cursed by God.

For a long time, I thought that the curse happened because Adam had listened to his wife—because of this line: "Because you have listened to the voice of your wife, and have eaten of the tree . . ." (Genesis 3:17). But as we look at the passage as a whole, a more accurate picture of Moses' authorial intent emerges: The emphasis is not on Eve but on the fact that Adam listened to the serpent *through* Eve and *instead of* God. Adam had been present when the serpent had tempted Eve (Genesis 3:6). It wasn't as if she relayed a message he'd never heard before. Adam knew what God had said and what the serpent said. And instead of listening to God, he listened to the serpent through Eve.

Listening to the wrong voice has dire consequences.

13. Write out Genesis 3:15. Who do you think "he" is?

Some Bible scholars refer to this verse as the protoevangelium, or the first reference in Scripture to the Messiah: Jesus, who would be the offspring of a woman who trusted God—Mary of Nazareth—and rescue the whole world from evil forces.

14. What unanswered questions do you have about the Garden of Eden or anything else you've read so far?

15. What encouraged you most in your reading?

> [Adam and Eve] take a shortcut, and what they gain when their eyes are opened is cheap knowledge: "They knew that they were naked" (3:7). Insight does not grow on trees.[4]
>
> **Ellen F. Davis, *Opening Israel's Scriptures***

A small group gathered at my home for several weeks as I was writing this Bible study, and we processed these lessons and questions together. For the people in my group, the most unsettling and confusing elements of this garden story were how quickly and easily Eve and Adam were deceived—and why the serpent was in the Garden in the first place. We found the presence of the Tree of the Knowledge of Good and Evil perplexing.

Feeling confused about something in the Bible is not a bad thing. It means you are learning, you're curious, and you have more studying to do. Christians are lifelong learners, always uncovering new and clarifying things about God.

Adam and Eve's sin wasn't having questions about God or his boundaries. After all, it was the serpent who raised the questions in the first place. It was that they took their confusion and doubt into their own hands instead of bringing those questions and doubts to God.

Don't hide your questions from God. Don't look for answers without him. God wants you to walk with him in the garden so you can discover just how trustworthy he is.

PART 3

UNDERSTANDING

Now that we've finished a close reading of the Scriptures, we're going to spend some time on interpretation: doing our best to understand what God was saying to the original audience and what he's teaching us through the process. But to do so, we need to learn his ways and consider how God's Word would have been understood by the original audience before applying the same truths to our own lives. "Scripture interpretation" may sound a little stuffy, but understanding what God means to communicate to us in the Bible is crucial to enjoying a close relationship with Jesus. Part 3 will enable you to answer the question *What does it mean?*

ADAM AND EVE'S POWER GRAB led to epic disappointment—paradise lost and potential squandered. Many of us recognize that feeling. Our lives feel like the Garden of Eden, brimming with potential but suffering the consequences of sinful choices. Or perhaps we know what it's like to disregard the Lord and choose instead to listen to people in our lives who don't have our best interests at heart, don't care about honoring the Lord, or are unaware that their recommendations are not God's best for our lives.

Reflecting on this first garden in Scripture should lead us to evaluate our own lives. For each question below, circle the applicable response.

Am I living up to my potential as God's image bearer?	Yes	No	Sometimes
Do I really know who I am?	Yes	No	Sometimes
Do I trust that God's boundaries are for my good?	Yes	No	Sometimes
Am I bringing God my questions and doubts?	Yes	No	Sometimes

These kinds of questions are the work of the Holy Spirit, who searches and knows our hearts and kindly, lovingly reveals the truth. Whatever it means for us—whether we have a lot of heartache to name and process or we are praying for the humility to repent of our resistance to God's wisdom—let's be brave enough to answer the Lord when he calls out our names and course corrects our exile-prone hearts.

Until I started researching the Garden of Eden, I hadn't paid much attention to biblical references to this garden beyond Genesis 2 and 3. However, the Old Testament mentions and alludes to the celestial garden of God in several places. Each reference adds dimension to our understanding of the Garden of Eden and how the reality of this place impacted God's people. They imagined Eden would be restored eventually.

1. **Read the three passages below and describe what you learn about the Garden of Eden from each Old Testament reference.**

13 So Abram went up from Egypt, he and his wife, and all that he had,
and Lot with him, into the Negeb.
2 Now Abram was very rich in livestock, in silver, and in gold. 3 He
journeyed on by stages from the Negeb as far as Bethel, to the place
where his tent had been at the beginning, between Bethel and Ai, 4 to
the place where he had made an altar at the first; and there Abram
called on the name of the LORD. 5 Now Lot, who went with Abram, also
had flocks and herds and tents, 6 so that the land could not support

both of them living together; for their possessions were so great that
they could not live together, 7 and there was strife between the herders
of Abram's livestock and the herders of Lot's livestock. At that time the
Canaanites and the Perizzites lived in the land.

8 Then Abram said to Lot, "Let there be no strife between you and
me, and between your herders and my herders; for we are kindred.
9 Is not the whole land before you? Separate yourself from me. If you
take the left hand, then I will go to the right; or if you take the right
hand, then I will go to the left." 10 Lot looked about him, and saw that
the plain of the Jordan was well watered everywhere like the garden
of the LORD, like the land of Egypt, in the direction of Zoar; this was
before the LORD had destroyed Sodom and Gomorrah. 11 So Lot chose
for himself all the plain of the Jordan, and Lot journeyed eastward; thus
they separated from each other. 12 Abram settled in the land of Canaan,
while Lot settled among the cities of the Plain and moved his tent as
far as Sodom. 13 Now the people of Sodom were wicked, great sinners
against the LORD.

GENESIS 13:1-13

2. What do you learn about the Garden of the Lord from Genesis 13:10?

For the LORD will comfort Zion;
he will comfort all her waste places,
and will make her wilderness like Eden,
her desert like the garden of the LORD;
joy and gladness will be found in her,
thanksgiving and the voice of song.

ISAIAH 51:3

3. **What do you learn about the Garden of the Lord from Isaiah 51:3?**

24 I will take you from the nations, and gather you from all the countries,
and bring you into your own land. 25 I will sprinkle clean water upon you,
and you shall be clean from all your uncleannesses, and from all your idols
I will cleanse you. 26 A new heart I will give you, and a new spirit I will put
within you; and I will remove from your body the heart of stone and give
you a heart of flesh. 27 I will put my spirit within you, and make you follow
my statutes and be careful to observe my ordinances. 28 Then you shall
live in the land that I gave to your ancestors; and you shall be my people,
and I will be your God. 29 I will save you from all your uncleannesses, and I
will summon the grain and make it abundant and lay no famine upon you.
30 I will make the fruit of the tree and the produce of the field abundant,
so that you may never again suffer the disgrace of famine among the
nations. 31 Then you shall remember your evil ways, and your dealings that
were not good; and you shall loathe yourselves for your iniquities and your

abominable deeds. [32] It is not for your sake that I will act, says the Lord GOD; let that be known to you. Be ashamed and dismayed for your ways, O house of Israel.

[33] Thus says the Lord GOD: On the day that I cleanse you from all your iniquities, I will cause the towns to be inhabited, and the waste places shall be rebuilt. [34] The land that was desolate shall be tilled, instead of being the desolation that it was in the sight of all who passed by. [35] And they will say, "This land that was desolate has become like the garden of Eden; and the waste and desolate and ruined towns are now inhabited and fortified." [36] Then the nations that are left all around you shall know that I, the LORD, have rebuilt the ruined places, and replanted that which was desolate; I, the LORD, have spoken, and I will do it.

EZEKIEL 36:24-36

4. What do you learn about the Garden of the Lord from Ezekiel 36:35?

If anything is clear from these Old Testament mentions of the Garden of the Lord, it is this: God can replant any garden. If you've noticed the familiar cycle happening in each of these texts, keep your chin up. Raise your gaze to God and let him fill you with hope. Yes, places like the Garden of Eden are prey to the serpent's trickery. Yes, people like you and me, and Adam and Eve, often fall into temptation and choose rebellion over devotion to God. But the good news is that even when the soil of our lives turns into a desert of dry, unlivable land, God can replant us.

5. What does the Lord want you to learn from these words from the prophet Isaiah?

> **3 [The LORD] will make her wilderness like Eden,**
> **and her desert like the garden of the LORD.**
>
> ISAIAH 51:3, CSB

All the places in the Bible where the Lord's presence dwells are connected to each other. The shared locations should bridge our imaginations from one part of the Bible to the next and reveal fresh insights about God. That's why we are going to spend some time thinking about how the Garden of Eden connects to other places where God's presence has dwelt among his people.

MAKING CONNECTIONS

An important part of understanding the meaning of a Bible passage is getting a sense of its place in the broader storyline of Scripture. When we make connections between different parts of the Bible, we get a glimpse of the unity and cohesion of the Scriptures.

God has always wanted to be with us. That's the beauty of the Garden of Eden, and it's also the reason behind the Tabernacle and the Temple. Each of those places was designed by God to be a place of meeting with him. Notice with me a pattern that emerges in Scripture:

- God comes to his people or comes to his people again.
- God creates a place to meet with his people.
- God's people don't trust God fully, and they reject his boundaries.
- God's people are exiled as a consequence of their sins.

The Tabernacle. Although Adam and Eve were expelled from the Garden of Eden, we see from the earliest stories of the Old Testament that because of God's great love for us, he still makes a way to commune with his people—even when we sin. That's why God came to Moses and the Israelites at Mount Sinai with instructions to build a Tabernacle, a new place to meet with him.[5] Sadly, even after building the Tabernacle and worshiping God there, God's people rebelled again, and they were exiled to wander in the wilderness for forty years.

The Temple. After God's people were finally settled in the Promised Land, God gave them instructions for the Temple in Jerusalem, a new place to meet with him. As you might predict, even after building and worshiping God in the Temple, God's people rebelled again, and thousands were exiled from their homelands under the oppression of the Assyrians and Babylonians. Even after the vicious cycle of sin repeated itself over and over, God graciously sent prophets to promise his people that one day he would bring them back to the Temple, that he would dwell with them.

The New Temple, Jesus. By the time we get to the New Testament, God's people expected a Messiah, a new king in the line of David who would restore Israel to Jerusalem, to bring them to the Temple to be with God. But Jesus came and told everyone that he is the new Temple. He's the new "place" who can help people commune with God—because he is God.

God loves us and wants to be in a self-sacrificing covenant relationship with us, and he will overcome any resistance, rebellion, or rejection from us. And he does so, time and time again, by providing a way for us to enjoy his presence. His love for us is so unconditional! He will continue to pursue us and invite us to walk alongside him, speak to him, bring him our questions and wonderings, and live in reliant trust in our Savior.

Notice with me some of the story elements the Garden of Eden and the Tabernacle share below.

THE GARDEN OF EDEN VS. THE TABERNACLE

Shared Literary Elements	The Garden of Eden (Genesis 1–3)	The Tabernacle (Exodus 25–30; 35–40)
Trees	The Tree of Life was in the Garden of Eden (Genesis 2:9).	Acacia wood was a significant part of the Tabernacle construction (Exodus 36:20).
Cherubim	Cherubim guarded the Garden of Eden when Adam and Eve were exiled (Genesis 3:24).	Two cherubim of gold faced each other across the mercy seat on the Ark of the Covenant (Exodus 25:18-22) and were features of the fabric for the Tabernacle (Exodus 26:1).
God's Presence	The Lord walked in the Garden of Eden to make his presence accessible to Adam and Eve (Genesis 3:8).	The Bread of the Presence was always before the Lord in the Tabernacle as a reminder that the Lord was always providing his presence (Exodus 25:30).
Vice-Regents	Adam and Eve were the garden cultivators commissioned by God to steward his creation together (Genesis 1:28).	The priests were the Tabernacle officiants commanded by God to facilitate worship (Exodus 28–29).
Clothes	In their naked shame, Adam and Eve needed to be clothed (Genesis 3:21).	The priests wore sacred vestments to participate in Tabernacle worship (Exodus 28).
Atonement	The first death in the fallen world was not of the guilty humans, Adam and Eve, but of an innocent animal, whose skin was used to clothe Adam and Eve. Blood was shed to cover their shame as a substitutionary atonement (Genesis 3:21).	Many animals were sacrificed in the Tabernacle to provide substitutionary atonement for the Israelites to enjoy God's covenant blessings (Exodus 29:38-46).
Gold	Gold was associated with the Garden of Eden (Genesis 2:12).	Gold was a feature of the Tabernacle (Exodus 26:6, 29, 35–37).

6. Read Exodus 29:38-46 and circle anything related to God's nearness to his people.

[38] Now this is what you shall offer on the altar: two lambs a year old
regularly each day. [39] One lamb you shall offer in the morning, and the
other lamb you shall offer in the evening; [40] and with the first lamb one-
tenth of a measure of choice flour mixed with one-fourth of a hin of
beaten oil, and one-fourth of a hin of wine for a drink offering. [41] And
the other lamb you shall offer in the evening, and shall offer with it a
grain offering and its drink offering, as in the morning, for a pleasing
odor, an offering by fire to the LORD. [42] It shall be a regular burnt offering
throughout your generations at the entrance of the tent of meeting
before the LORD, where I will meet with you, to speak to you there. [43] I will
meet with the Israelites there, and it shall be sanctified by my glory; [44] I
will consecrate the tent of meeting and the altar; Aaron also and his sons
I will consecrate, to serve me as priests. [45] I will dwell among the Israelites,
and I will be their God. [46] And they shall know that I am the LORD their
God, who brought them out of the land of Egypt that I might dwell among
them; I am the LORD their God.

EXODUS 29:38-46

7. What stands out to you about God's relationship with his people?

8. What implications does that have for your relationship with God?

Without God's staying presence, we'd all be stuck in our failures. But God faithfully continues to be available to us, to be with us in our pain, suffering, rebellion, expulsion, and exile. He is with us.

- If God needs to plant us in a garden to be with us, he will.
- If he needs to provide the blueprints for a Tabernacle and later a Temple to be with us, he will.
- And if he needs to come embodied as a human Temple, as Jesus, he will.

In the meantime, God invites all of us to turn to him, to talk to him, and ultimately to trust him.

Maybe you just need to be reminded that God is not like the friends who have ghosted and dropped us. God is not like the loved ones who have abandoned us. God stays. He never leaves. God will make a way to connect with us no matter how far we wander, no matter where exile takes us. He's close to you now, even as you read. You can count on him. God is ever present, accessible, available, and eager to enjoy your company.

9. Write God a thank-you note for his staying presence.

In every lesson, we'll expand our storyline chart to trace the garden locations we are studying together.

THE GARDENS STORYLINE OF SCRIPTURE

Location	Scripture(s)	The Presence of God
The Garden of Eden	Genesis 1–3	God walked with Adam and Eve in the Garden of Eden.
The Garden of Ahasuerus	Esther 1, 7	God was working behind the scenes to save his people.
The Garden of Gethsemane	Matthew 26	Christ agonized over his impending crucifixion.
The Gardens of the Crucifixion and Resurrection	John 19–20	Christ appeared to Mary Magdalene and commissioned her to tell the other disciples of his resurrection.
The Garden City	Revelation 21–22	God will come to dwell with his people.

The Protection of God	The Provision of God	The Produce of God
God did not let Adam and Eve live forever in a fallen world.	God provided substitutionary atonement.	God planted the Tree of Life.
God did not let Haman's plan come to fruition.	God gave Esther and Mordecai courage.	God planted Esther in the Garden of Ahasuerus so she could ask the king to save the Jewish people.
God does not require us to die as a consequence of our sin, because Jesus willingly gave his life to save ours.	Christ gave Christians his life.	Jesus is the Vine, and we are the branches.
Christ paid the penalty for our sins on the cross.	Christ rose from the dead, securing our future resurrection.	Jesus' resurrection foreshadows the resurrection of all believers in Christ.
God will wipe away all the tears from our eyes.	God will make all things new.	God will plant a new Garden City.

1. **What about the Garden of Eden story resonates with you most? What part of the story piques your curiosity?**

2. **What did you learn about God in this lesson? And what did you learn about yourself in this lesson?**

3. **How should these truths shape your faith community and change you?**

PART 4

RESPONDING

The purpose of Bible study is to help you become more Christlike; that's why part 4 will include journaling space for your reflection on and responses to the content and a blank checklist for actionable next steps. You'll be able to process what you're learning so that you can live out the concepts and pursue Christlikeness. Part 4 will enable you to answer the questions *What truths is this passage teaching?* and *How do I apply this to my life?*

IT'S NO SECRET that I'm a wimpy wilderness girl. I often joke that hotels are my camping. And the few times my husband, Aaron, has tried to plan an outdoor "adventure" for our family, I've jokingly responded, "Are you trying to kill us?" (Obviously, there are no other reasons to go into the wilderness. The choices are stay safe at a hotel or die.)

That same reaction came up in me when I first read about the Garden of Eden. Why did God let the serpent into the garden, anyway? Why did he threaten their lives if they ate from the wrong tree? Was he trying to kill Adam and Eve? Does God want us to die?

If I assume that God is trying to kill us off like unwanted weeds, I might misjudge God's intentions, question his sovereignty, and resent his mercy. But if God is good; if he's on a mission is to give us the abundant, fruitful life; if he is willing to give his own life to secure the abundant, fruitful life he intends for us to live—well, that God I can trust. That God does not want us to die. He is the Way and the Truth and the Life. I'll still question him. But my questions will be void of suspicion. Instead, if I bring what I know to be true about God's loving-kindness and faithfulness, I will begin to see in the Garden of Eden narratives a God who just won't quit us. A God who invites us to bring him our curiosity instead of turning to other sources for answers and to trust that the boundaries he's set for us are for our good and our growth.

Below are some of my reflections on the Scriptures we've read together. I hope they encourage you.

1. YOU CAN TRUST GOD'S BOUNDARIES.

God has the very best reserved for you. You can trust him. He's not throwing you into a pit of vipers or leaving you to wander the deserts of sin alone. God, with great care, intentionally planted you in your family, in your neighborhood, in your workplace, in your friend group for a great purpose: to be a good gardener. The kind of gardener who reflects the good Gardener. He's not like the serpent, tricky and deceiving. God wants you to flourish.

Some of us need to rip up some terrible theology from our lives, stuff that doesn't have anything to do with the boundaries God has given us. We need to root out weeds of doubt about God's goodness. Right this very minute, you need to trash the enemy's lie that God is not on your side. Trash the idea that God is waiting for you to fail. Heap those words of death into the pit of hell, where they belong. You were created by the loving Creator to cultivate his love in the world. You were born to grow. Whatever is holding you back from growth, ditch it. God wants you to trust his boundaries.

2. TRUSTING GOD'S BOUNDARIES GROWS THE KINGDOM.

You and I do not flourish in our faith for our benefit alone. Our growth is supposed to multiply. Just like Adam and Eve, God's garden stewards, we're commissioned to be fruitful and multiply. You are mission critical, as my friend Nika likes to say. I think a bunch of us are timid in our faith because we're convinced that only a select few Christians are the grow-things people. As if somehow some of us are the B team for God's Kingdom. I don't know how that lie slithered into our lives, but it's got to go. Send your persistent imposter syndrome to Hades. And make sure to bundle that trash with the residual effects of rejection and feelings of insignificance. You are on God's A team. You're his first choice. Your playing small is an affront to the good Gardener. Shrinking like a wilted flower is the cowardice the enemy wants to see multiply in your life.

But there is another way to live. You have been called by God Almighty to be his disciple, following Jesus, the Vine, and bearing much good fruit like any good growing plant would do. Why? So you can pile up some good works like a stack of ripe fruit? No. God wants your trust so that you can bless others. Go live up to your potential.

3. GOD WANTS YOU TO GROW THINGS HE PLANTS.

I know what you're thinking: *Growing things sounds hard.* And maybe that's why so many of us never even try to grow up in our faith or branch out to reach others with our fruit. Here's the thing: God is the One doing the planting. We don't have to worry or psych ourselves out of faithful acts of obedience because of some nonsense about the work of cultivation being too hard. Yes, our growth and the work of growing things are going to require resistance. How else will our roots grow deep and our branches sturdy? But if you are concerned about how growing things is going to happen, you can take a long, deep breath of relief. That's not your concern. God does the planting. He's the ultimate Gardener. Yes, we reflect him, but we are not him. I have a sneaking suspicion that most of our failed attempts to grow the things he's called us to cultivate happen because we are struggling to trust him. Let's trust him to do *his* work so we can focus on ours. God wants you to grow things, but don't forget—he wants you to grow the things he's planted.

Use this journaling space to process what you are learning.

Ask yourself how these truths impact your relationship with God and with others.

What is the Holy Spirit bringing to your mind as actionable next steps in your faith journey?

- ✿
- ✿
- ✿

LESSON TWO

TRUSTING CHRIST'S KINGSHIP

**THE GARDEN OF AHASUERUS:
A DRUNKEN KING'S BANQUET**

SCRIPTURE: ESTHER 1, 7

PART 1

CONTEXT

Before you begin your study, we will start with the context of the story we are about to read together: the setting, both cultural and historical; the people involved; and where our passage fits in the larger setting of Scripture. All these things help us make sense of what we're reading. Understanding the context of a Bible story is fundamental to reading Scripture well. Getting your bearings before you read will enable you to answer the question *What am I about to read?*

WE DO STRANGE THINGS with women in the Bible.

- *Villains.* Often, we cast them as villains, and we have the common interpretation of Eve to blame for that. Eve's role in the Garden of Eden might tempt us to perceive her as a temptress, a scoundrel, a usurper. But what if she was genuinely trying to help Adam become wise? What if she and Adam together responded to the serpent and she just happened to be the one to share the forbidden fruit? The assumptions we make about Eve can color how we see all the other women in Scripture.
- *Vixens.* Sometimes we cast them as vixens. Many early church fathers and even modern preachers label the woman at the well (John 4:1-42) and the woman with the alabaster jar (Luke 7:36-50) as prostitutes, but there's no

evidence in the Bible to support those theories. We usually assume both women were fallen, inappropriate; but given the lack of information in the text, both could just as easily have been wealthy, influential figures in their communities.[1]

- *Princesses.* Conversely, sometimes we imagine women in the Bible as pretty, pretty princesses rather than the heroines in very dark and serious adventure stories. This frequently happens with Esther, the orphaned Jewish girl who rescued the Jewish people from extinction in Persia. Instead of seeing Esther as a new Joseph leading her people into favor with a foreign king, we talk about Esther as a young bride waiting for her Prince Charming.

Obviously, not all women in the Bible were "good." Plenty of female biblical figures were downright evil. But for the women who were valiant and devoted to their faith, sometimes we replace their presence in the text with some warped version of their reality. Our interpretations of women in the Bible reveal a lot about our capacity to dignify women in the text *and* in our world today.

I've been guilty of all these readings of women in the Bible. But most often, I've just overlooked their presence in the text altogether, focusing on the more popular male Bible heroes. Not until the last decade have I intentionally studied Bible women. I've been shocked to find that these women played diverse and indispensable roles in God's story:

- Miriam, the prophetess and worship leader of Israel;
- Deborah, the commander of the Israelite army, a prophetess, and the judge in charge of the nation;
- The woman at the well, the first evangelist in John's Gospel;
- Mary Magdalene, the first gospel preacher; and
- Lydia of Philippi, the first church planter in Europe.

We can far too easily neglect any attention the Lord gave these inspiring sheroes of our faith and focus instead only on the amazing male heroes in the

Bible. As I've tried to pay more attention to women in Scripture, the book of Esther has piqued my curiosity. The title alone signals Esther's importance in biblical history. Just like Ruth, Esther needed a whole book of the Bible devoted to her valor.

Honest to goodness, I used to picture Esther as a Disney princess . . . which goes to show how little of the book of Esther I had really studied. Although God is never directly mentioned in the book of Esther, he's implied throughout the whole scroll as the sovereign God of the universe who's mindful of his commitment to the Jewish people and powerful enough to save them. This book is filled with themes like divine sovereignty, human responsibility, civil disobedience, feasting and fasting, and female agency.

But there is no story about Esther's bravery without a story about the defiant woman she replaced: Queen Vashti.[2] And the backdrop of Vashti's story? The Garden of Ahasuerus.

Vashti's and Esther's stories happen during the reign of Ahasuerus (better known as Xerxes) as king of Persia. At this time in history, the Israelites were living as exiles in Persia. After finally reaching the Promised Land, God's people hadn't honored the Lord. They'd stopped listening to God, trusting God—and the consequences had been exile from the Promised Land and captivity in a foreign land, Babylon (later called Persia). Sound familiar?

A lot had happened to the Israelites since the exodus from Egypt, but one storyline that shows up in the book of Esther is the Israelites' conflict with the Amalekites. Since leaving Egypt, Israel had fought several battles against many different enemies, but one of the longest conflicts happened to be with the Amalekites—at least one of whom, Haman, was in leadership in Persia during King Ahasuerus's reign. It is against this backdrop that the book of Esther was written.

The book of Esther is full of literary connections to the rest of the Old Testament. I've repurposed the brilliant work of Drs. Longman and Dillard, who do an excellent job summarizing the Bible scholarship done by others, into a chart to give you a visual representation of the literary connections between Esther and the Exodus, Moses, and Joseph, respectively.[3]

OLD TESTAMENT LITERARY CONNECTIONS IN THE BOOK OF ESTHER

Esther and the Exodus	both stories . . . • are set in foreign lands • focus on threats against the Jews • detail the deliverance of God's people and vengeance against their enemies • end with the institution of an annual Jewish festival
Esther and Moses	both characters . . . • are adopted • withhold their identities for a time • fight against the Amalekites
Esther and Joseph	both stories . . . • involve "the disturbed sleep of the monarch" both characters . . . • are Jewish heroes • "rise to prominence in a foreign court" • are "in contact with royal officials" • reveal their Jewish identities in a banquet scene • "become the means by which the Jews are saved"

God inspired the writers of Scripture to repeat literary themes and pivotal imagery, which means that God wants us to read the book of Esther in light of all the other Old Testament books, in light of the exile from the Garden of Eden, and in light of the rescue of God's people through the Exodus. And perhaps most importantly, God wants us to notice that the King of the Garden of Eden is nothing like the king of the garden in the book of Esther. In fact, King Ahasuerus is more like the serpent from the Garden of Eden—inviting a woman into temptation in the presence of her husband.

Here we have a dysfunctional couple who exemplify a battle of the sexes: Queen Vashti and King Ahasuerus. They seem to live into the reality given to Adam and Eve after the Fall—that men and women, who were supposed to complement one another, are now in competition. And, like the Garden of Eden, King Ahasuerus's garden is a setting with a couple; a very real enemy; and a plot about temptation, defiance, and banishment.

It was never supposed to be this way. Never. The battle of the sexes was not

God's original design for men and women. Vashti and Ahasuerus will show us as much. The sons of Adam and the daughters of Eve need to find their way to a new garden where God dwells and longs for restored relationship, not just between them and him but also between men and women.

My prayer is that reading about the Garden of Ahasuerus will evoke in us a visceral response to the brokenness sin can cause in our relationships and our world—not so that we can revel in the pain or trauma bond with a character in Scripture but so that we can process through the failures of the fallen and move on into hope. A new King has come, a new garden is in our future, and all this mess around us will be made right one day.

> Without explicitly didactic narration, Esther 1 compares Ahasuerus's focus on externals of the kingdom's trappings (vv. 4, 6) with the beauty of his own wife (v. 11), equating them as pretty property fit for consumption on demand. But Vashti's refusal to appear demonstrated that, whether for good or for ill, Vashti saw herself as more than just a pretty face.[4]
>
> **Sharifa Stevens, "Vashti," in *Vindicating the Vixens***

---

1. **PERSONAL CONTEXT: What is going on in your life right now that might impact how you understand the Garden of Ahasuerus story? What do you hope to learn from this lesson?**

2. **SPIRITUAL CONTEXT: If you've never studied the Garden of Ahasuerus before, what piques your curiosity? If you've studied this place or the book of Esther before, what impressions and insights do you recall?**

3. **BIBLICAL CONTEXT: What questions come to mind as you read about the context of Esther and the Garden of Ahasuerus? What questions do you wish you could have answered before studying this part of Scripture?**

PART 2

SEEING

Seeing the text is vital if we want the heart of the Scripture passage to sink in. We read slowly and intentionally through the text with the context in mind. As we practice close, thoughtful reading of Scripture, we pick up on phrases, implications, and meanings we might otherwise have missed. Part 2 includes close Scripture reading and observation questions to empower you to answer the question *What is the story saying?*

1. Read Esther 1 and circle any references to Queen Vashti.

1 This happened in the days of Ahasuerus, the same Ahasuerus who
ruled over one hundred twenty-seven provinces from India to Ethiopia.
2 In those days when King Ahasuerus sat on his royal throne in the citadel
of Susa, 3 in the third year of his reign, he gave a banquet for all his
officials and ministers. The army of Persia and Media and the nobles and
governors of the provinces were present, 4 while he displayed the great
wealth of his kingdom and the splendor and pomp of his majesty for many
days, one hundred eighty days in all.

5 When these days were completed, the king gave for all the people
present in the citadel of Susa, both great and small, a banquet lasting for
seven days, in the court of the garden of the king's palace. 6 There were

white cotton curtains and blue hangings tied with cords of fine linen and
purple to silver rings and marble pillars. There were couches of gold and
silver on a mosaic pavement of porphyry, marble, mother-of-pearl,
and colored stones. [7] Drinks were served in golden goblets, goblets of
different kinds, and the royal wine was lavished according to the bounty
of the king. [8] Drinking was by flagons, without restraint; for the king had
given orders to all the officials of his palace to do as each one desired.
[9] Furthermore, Queen Vashti gave a banquet for the women in the palace
of King Ahasuerus.

[10] On the seventh day, when the king was merry with wine, he
commanded Mehuman, Biztha, Harbona, Bigtha and Abagtha, Zethar
and Carkas, the seven eunuchs who attended him, [11] to bring Queen Vashti
before the king, wearing the royal crown, in order to show the peoples and
the officials her beauty; for she was fair to behold. [12] But Queen Vashti
refused to come at the king's command conveyed by the eunuchs. At this
the king was enraged, and his anger burned within him.

[13] Then the king consulted the sages who knew the laws (for this was
the king's procedure toward all who were versed in law and custom, [14] and
those next to him were Carshena, Shethar, Admatha, Tarshish, Meres,
Marsena, and Memucan, the seven officials of Persia and Media, who
had access to the king, and sat first in the kingdom): [15] "According to the
law, what is to be done to Queen Vashti because she has not performed
the command of King Ahasuerus conveyed by the eunuchs?" [16] Then
Memucan said in the presence of the king and the officials, "Not only has
Queen Vashti done wrong to the king, but also to all the officials and all
the peoples who are in all the provinces of King Ahasuerus. [17] For this
deed of the queen will be made known to all women, causing them to look
with contempt on their husbands, since they will say, 'King Ahasuerus
commanded Queen Vashti to be brought before him, and she did not
come.' [18] This very day the noble ladies of Persia and Media who have
heard of the queen's behavior will rebel against the king's officials, and
there will be no end of contempt and wrath! [19] If it pleases the king, let a

royal order go out from him, and let it be written among the laws of the Persians and the Medes so that it may not be altered, that Vashti is never again to come before King Ahasuerus; and let the king give her royal position to another who is better than she.
20 So when the decree made by the king is proclaimed throughout all his kingdom, vast as it is, all women will give honor to their husbands, high and low alike."

21 This advice pleased the king and the officials, and the king did as Memucan proposed;
22 he sent letters to all the royal provinces, to every province in its own script and to every people in its own language, declaring that every man should be master in his own house.

ESTHER 1

2. **Make a bulleted list of everything you learn about Queen Vashti from Esther 1.**

3. **Based on the author's clues about the Garden of King Ahasuerus, how would you describe this garden to a friend? Write your answer below.**

4. What elements in Esther 1 remind you of the Garden of Eden?

In the Ancient Near East, including in Persia, the king's palace complex often included a large "gazebo-style pavilion."[5] This pavilion was "reserved for royal use" and surrounded by a private garden that was full of fruit and shade trees, kind of like a park or an arboretum.[6]

This building [the pavilion] was often surrounded by a private garden planted with fruit trees and shade trees, with watercourses, pools and paths—more like a park. Its arboretum often contained many exotic trees and plants. Such gardens have been excavated at Pasargadae, Cyrus the Great's capital city.[7]

John H. Walton, Victor H. Matthews, and Mark W. Chavalas, "Esther," in *The IVP Bible Background Commentary: Old Testament*

---

5. Why did Queen Vashti's refusal cause such a stir? Based on Esther 1:17–18, what were the power players worried about?

It's clear that the men of Persia were counting on a legal decree to rein in rebellious women and ensure that wives honored their husbands. The poetic irony is that the entire book of Esther could be summed up as female civil disobedience. But it's not civil disobedience intended to further the divide between the sexes. When Esther and Vashti rebelled—though they didn't necessarily do it with the same motive—they ultimately preserved the honor of King Ahasuerus. Parading a spouse before a group of drunken men does not honor the king, and neither does mass genocide.

6. Based on Esther 1:19, what was Vashti's punishment for refusing the king?

Ahasuerus was revealed as a man more concerned about showing off to his man-crowd than protecting his wife. The author of Esther demonstrates how the godless treat their women—as sex objects, as disposable—by casting the one who should be the figure of honor, Ahasuerus, the *king*, as the most loathsome example. He became a symbol of lusty caprice. And his ability to control his household, his subjects, or his kingdom, hung on the gallows with Haman. Esther's will was done, however, because the *genuine* figure of honor was Yahweh, and he, through providence, exalted Esther at every turn. Yahweh was and is the true king.[8]

Sharifa Stevens, "Vashti," in *Vindicating the Vixens*

The last two verses in this chapter gave me a good chuckle. The king sent a letter to ensure that the women in his kingdom wouldn't treat their husbands the way he'd been treated. An ominous entourage of eunuchs couldn't force Vashti to obey, but a letter would get all the women around the kingdom in line? The Persian Empire's dispatch system was famous for helping news travel fast.[9]

Can you imagine the betrayal Vashti must have felt after being rejected? This disgrace wouldn't be kept a secret, and everyone in the kingdom would know about Vashti's demotion quickly. She likely watched as her replacements were paraded through the palace on their way to the king's bedroom.

After my first reading of the text, I just kept writing *What?!?!* in the margins of my Bible. I love hosting—I really do. But I can't fathom hosting this many people for this long. And this wasn't hosting at all; it was a way for the king to show off his wealth. And his wife.

The Bible has a lot to say about how a righteous king should behave. While several verses in Proverbs affirm the expectations a kingdom should have of a sober-minded king, none are so direct as King Lemuel's words from his mother, which he repeats in Proverbs 31.

7. Referencing Proverbs 31:1-9, list some ways King Ahasuerus missed the mark.

31 **The words of King Lemuel. An oracle that his mother taught him:**

2 No, my son! No, son of my womb!
No, son of my vows!
3 Do not give your strength to women,
your ways to those who destroy kings.
4 It is not for kings, O Lemuel,
it is not for kings to drink wine,
or for rulers to desire strong drink;
5 or else they will drink and forget what has been decreed,
and will pervert the rights of all the afflicted.

[6] Give strong drink to one who is perishing,
and wine to those in bitter distress;
[7] let them drink and forget their poverty,
and remember their misery no more.
[8] Speak out for those who cannot speak,
for the rights of all the destitute.
[9] Speak out, judge righteously,
defend the rights of the poor and needy.

PROVERBS 31:1-9

✿

✿

✿

8. What unanswered questions do you have about the Garden of Ahasuerus or anything else you've read so far?

9. What encouraged you most in your reading?

The Garden of Ahasuerus is an antigarden in Scripture—the antithesis of connection to God and rootedness in flourishing relationship. It was never supposed to be this way. The author of Esther makes it clear: The idyllic dream of Eden had turned into a nightmare.

PART 3

UNDERSTANDING

Now that we've finished a close reading of the Scriptures, we're going to spend some time on interpretation: doing our best to understand what God was saying to the original audience and what he's teaching us through the process. But to do so, we need to learn his ways and consider how God's Word would have been understood by the original audience before applying the same truths to our own lives. "Scripture interpretation" may sound a little stuffy, but understanding what God means to communicate to us in the Bible is crucial to enjoying a close relationship with Jesus. Part 3 will enable you to answer the question *What does it mean?*

DESPITE ALL OUR FAILED ATTEMPTS to quit God, he doesn't quit us.

Since the Garden of Eden, the enemy has continued to tempt and distract God's people away from obedience and into rebellion. As a result of that first time, Adam and Eve experienced the consequences of their sins—namely, separation from God. The same is true for us today.

But God is unyielding in his unconditional, unfailing love. God didn't abandon his people after the Garden of Eden. He still provided everything they needed to cultivate creation and flourish in his presence. He continues to pursue us and offers us forgiveness and restoration. He did this after Adam and Eve were expelled from the Garden of Eden, after his people escaped from Egypt, after they were exiled from the Promised Land, and when they faced the threat of extinction in Persia. He's so wonderfully predictable. He is for his people, and he will stop at nothing to save us from ourselves.

In this lesson, we're going to put the Garden of Eden and the Garden of Ahasuerus side by side for comparison so that we can interpret Vashti's story. God's storytelling is masterful. The fallen Garden of Ahasuerus shows us what has happened to our relationships because humans have turned away from trusting God—but in showing us that, it also reveals that healthy, mutually respectful, honoring relationships between men and women are part of what God intends for our flourishing.

1. **Read Genesis 1:1-2 and Esther 1:1-3. Underline any time markers and circle any actions by God or King Ahasuerus.**

1 In the beginning when God created the heavens and the earth, [2] the earth was a formless void and darkness covered the face of the deep, while a wind from God swept over the face of the waters.

GENESIS 1:1-2

1 This happened in the days of Ahasuerus, the same Ahasuerus who ruled over one hundred twenty-seven provinces from India to Ethiopia. [2] In those days when King Ahasuerus sat on his royal throne in the citadel of Susa, [3] in the third year of his reign, he gave a banquet for all his officials and ministers.

ESTHER 1:1-3

Right from the start, we should see these two garden narratives as origin stories with time stamps. God Almighty was and is and always will be. King Ahasuerus had a beginning and an end. Ahasuerus only reigned for a few years in one kingdom made up of 127 provinces on one side of the world. God is the ruler of all kingdoms everywhere. God doesn't just sit on his royal throne; he hovered over the waters of the earth to commence his creation process. Our God is not idle or lazy. He is active and intentional.

2. **How do you imagine an ancient reader of the Old Testament would have interpreted the connection points between these two kings?**

3. **Read Genesis 1:26-28 and Esther 1:2-4. Underline the activity of God and King Ahasuerus and the purpose behind their actions.**

26 Then God said, "Let us make humankind in our image, according to our likeness; and let them have dominion over the fish of the sea, and over the birds of the air, and over the cattle, and over all the wild animals of the earth, and over every creeping thing that creeps upon the earth."

27 So God created humankind in
his image,
in the image of God he created
them;
male and female he created them.

28 God blessed them, and God said to them, "Be fruitful and multiply, and fill the earth and subdue it; and have dominion over the fish of the sea and over the birds of the air and over every living thing that moves upon the earth."

GENESIS 1:26-28

2 In those days when King
Ahasuerus sat on his royal
throne in the citadel of Susa,
3 in the third year of his reign,
he gave a banquet for all his
officials and ministers. The
army of Persia and Media and
the nobles and governors of the
provinces were present, 4 while
he displayed the great wealth
of his kingdom and the splendor
and pomp of his majesty for
many days, one hundred eighty
days in all.

ESTHER 1:2-4

What did King Ahasuerus do with his dominion and royal power? He partied. He partied to show off his riches and impress the leaders in his kingdom. In sharp contrast, the King of the original garden chose to share his power with Adam and Eve so that they could rule the earth as his vice-regents. While King Ahasuerus amassed a crowd to celebrate his incomparable majesty, God deputized the first humans to reflect his glory and bear his image. King Ahasuerus wanted all eyes on him and, soon, on Vashti. God wanted to empower people like Adam and Eve to reflect his likeness to others.

4. How would you describe the difference between God's motivations and King Ahasuerus's motivations?

5. Read Genesis 2:1–3 and Esther 1:5. Underline what God and King Ahasuerus do in these verses.

2 Thus the heavens and the
earth were finished, and all their
multitude. [2] And on the seventh day
God finished the work that he had
done, and he rested on the seventh
day from all the work that he had
done. [3] So God blessed the seventh
day and hallowed it, because on it
God rested from all the work that
he had done in creation.

GENESIS 2:1–3

[5] When these days were
completed, the king gave for all
the people present in the citadel
of Susa, both great and small, a
banquet lasting for seven days,
in the court of the garden of the
king's palace.

ESTHER 1:5

After drinking and partying for 180 days, King Ahasuerus did not sleep it off; he hosted another banquet. What? But this time the banquet was smaller and in the garden of the palace.

What did God do after creating for six days? He rested.

6. Read Genesis 2:15-17 and Esther 1:8. Circle anything that has to do with limits or a lack thereof.

15 The LORD God took the man and put him in the garden of Eden to till it and keep it. 16 And the LORD God commanded the man, "You may freely eat of every tree of the garden; 17 but of the tree of the knowledge of good and evil you shall not eat, for in the day that you eat of it you shall die."

GENESIS 2:15-17

8 Drinking was by flagons, without restraint; for the king had given orders to all the officials of his palace to do as each one desired.

ESTHER 1:8

God's garden had one limit, one rule: Do not eat from the Tree of the Knowledge of Good and Evil. And Adam and Eve couldn't resist the temptation from the serpent to rebel against God. But King Ahasuerus ordered his key leaders in the palace to do whatever they liked. You don't have to be a detective to pick up on the ominous undertones of this scene.

7. Read Genesis 2:18, 21-23 and Esther 1:10-11. Place a box around anything that has to do with the movement of a woman in either narrative.

18 Then the LORD God said, "It is
not good that the man should be
alone; I will make him a helper as
his partner." . . . 21 So the LORD God
caused a deep sleep to fall upon
the man, and he slept; then he
took one of his ribs and closed up
its place with flesh. 22 And the rib
that the LORD God had taken from
the man he made into a woman
and brought her to the man.
23 Then the man said,

"This at last is bone of my bones
    and flesh of my flesh;
this one shall be called Woman,
    for out of Man this one was
        taken."

GENESIS 2:18, 21-23

10 On the seventh day, when the
king was merry with wine, he
commanded Mehuman, Biztha,
Harbona, Bigtha and Abagtha,
Zethar and Carkas, the seven
eunuchs who attended him, 11 to
bring Queen Vashti before the
king, wearing the royal crown, in
order to show the peoples and
the officials her beauty; for she
was fair to behold.

ESTHER 1:10-11

God placed Adam in the Garden of Eden and created Adam and Eve to be corresponding allies in their cultivation and dominion work. God brought Eve to Adam not so that he could wield his authority over her but so that she could receive a name, a sign of relationship and partnership. But in Vashti's story, the king commanded the eunuchs to bring Queen Vashti into the palace garden to be at best admired and flaunted as property—and at worst preyed upon and commodified.

8. Read Genesis 3:6-7 and Esther 1:12. Note anything that the women in the story are doing.

[6] So when the woman saw that the tree was good for food, and that it was a delight to the eyes, and that the tree was to be desired to make one wise, she took of its fruit and ate; and she also gave some to her husband, who was with her, and he ate. [7] Then the eyes of both were opened, and they knew that they were naked; and they sewed fig leaves together and made loincloths for themselves.

GENESIS 3:6-7

[12] But Queen Vashti refused to come at the king's command conveyed by the eunuchs. At this the king was enraged, and his anger burned within him.

ESTHER 1:12

Eve listened to the serpent instead of God, taking the forbidden fruit and sharing it with her husband. Queen Vashti, on the other hand, did not listen to the eunuchs, did not take the bait, and refused her husband's request. We should feel some narrative tension between these two garden scenes.

9. Read Genesis 3:16 and Esther 1:19-22. Underline any oracles or decrees pronounced.

[16] To the woman he said,

"I will greatly increase your pangs
in childbearing;
in pain you shall bring forth
children,
yet your desire shall be for your
husband,
and he shall rule over you."

GENESIS 3:16

[19] "If it pleases the king, let a royal order go out from him, and let it be written among the laws of the Persians and the Medes so that it may not be altered, that Vashti is never again to come before King Ahasuerus; and let the king give her royal position to another who is better than she. [20] So when the decree made by the king is proclaimed throughout all his kingdom, vast as it is, all women will give honor to their husbands, high and low alike."

[21] This advice pleased the king and the officials, and the king did as Memucan proposed; [22] he sent letters to all the royal provinces, to every province in its own script and to every people in its own language, declaring that every man should be master in his own house.

ESTHER 1:19-22

Both Eve and Vashti had impacts on other women. Eve's failure resulted in a stratified hierarchy of male and female relationships and increased the pain of childbirth for all other women. Women went from complements to competition. Queen Vashti's protest influenced new legislation that repressed women, banning them from challenging their husbands. No longer were women allowed to live in their created role of *ʿēzer*, helper, voice of clarity and conviction working with one's husband for the good of the world. What started as an oracle in Eden was now a law in Persia.

Thanks a lot, ladies!

Eve was forced out of the Garden of Eden, and Vashti was forced out of the garden of the royal palace. Eve was demoted, and so was Queen Vashti. Their punishment was banishment and distance from the king. Neither woman would have access to the throne anymore; the Garden of Eden was guarded by cherubim, and the palace garden was guarded by eunuchs.

I hope you noticed what King Ahasuerus thought he could legislate: honor. No one can legislate honor. You can demand and enforce allegiance. You can punish dissenters, you can silence and disempower the defiant, but you can't make someone honor another person. We give honor to those we respect. To those with honorable lives.

The tragic irony is that King Ahasuerus should have listened to his wife. When she refused him, it should have been a warning signal that he'd taken things too far. He'd crossed the line. Instead, he listened to the wrong voices: his own drunken rage and the ill advice of his cowardly friends. This garden echoes Eden: Turning to our own preferences, living apart from the God who is trustworthy, harms our relationships and our ability to flourish.

MAKING CONNECTIONS

An important part of understanding the meaning of a Bible passage is getting a sense of its place in the broader storyline of Scripture. When we make connections between different parts of the Bible, we get a glimpse of the unity and cohesion of the Scriptures.

A lot happens between Vashti's dismissal in Esther 1 and the second time the Garden of Ahasuerus is mentioned in the book (in Esther 7). If you have time, read Esther 2–6 to prepare for this part of the lesson.

- **ESTHER 2 (ESTHER BECOMES QUEEN):**[10] An orphaned Jewish girl named Esther is taken into the king's harem. She pleases the king and is chosen as his new queen. We don't have time in this lesson to dig into the messed-up world young virgins like Esther had to navigate. What she would have had to go through to gain the king's affection makes my skin crawl.
- **ESTHER 3 (HAMAN UNDERTAKES TO DESTROY THE JEWS):** An evil leader named Haman rises up and devises a plan to wipe out the Jewish people.
- **ESTHER 4 (ESTHER AGREES TO HELP THE JEWS):** Esther's relative, Mordecai, uncovers Haman's plan and recruits Esther to help him save their people from destruction. Mordecai says that it is for such a time as this that God has elevate Esther into leadership, and she decides to risk her life to save her people.
- **ESTHER 5 (ESTHER'S BANQUET):** Esther puts her life on the line to save the Jewish people by getting the king's attention and appealing to him—an act of defiance not dissimilar to Vashti's refusal to obey his command.
- **ESTHER 6 (THE KING HONORS MORDECAI):** The king publicly commends Mordecai for thwarting an assassination attempt.

10. Read Esther 6:14–7:10. Circle any mention of a garden and underline everything Esther says in the story.

14 While [Haman's friends and family] were still talking with him, the king's
eunuchs arrived and hurried Haman off to the banquet that Esther had
prepared.

7 So the king and Haman went in to feast with Queen Esther. 2 On
the second day, as they were drinking wine, the king again said to Esther,
"What is your petition, Queen Esther? It shall be granted you. And what
is your request? Even to the half of my kingdom, it shall be fulfilled."

[3] Then Queen Esther answered, "If I have won your favor, O king, and
if it pleases the king, let my life be given me—that is my petition—and
the lives of my people—that is my request. [4] For we have been sold, I
and my people, to be destroyed, to be killed, and to be annihilated. If
we had been sold merely as slaves, men and women, I would have held
my peace; but no enemy can compensate for this damage to the king."
[5] Then King Ahasuerus said to Queen Esther, "Who is he, and where
is he, who has presumed to do this?" [6] Esther said, "A foe and enemy,
this wicked Haman!" Then Haman was terrified before the king and
the queen. [7] The king rose from the feast in wrath and went into the
palace garden, but Haman stayed to beg his life from Queen Esther,
for he saw that the king had determined to destroy him. [8] When the
king returned from the palace garden to the banquet hall, Haman
had thrown himself on the couch where Esther was reclining; and the
king said, "Will he even assault the queen in my presence, in my own
house?" As the words left the mouth of the king, they covered Haman's
face. [9] Then Harbona, one of the eunuchs in attendance on the king,
said, "Look, the very gallows that Haman has prepared for Mordecai,
whose word saved the king, stands at Haman's house, fifty cubits
high." And the king said, "Hang him on that." [10] So they hanged Haman
on the gallows that he had prepared for Mordecai. Then the anger of
the king abated.

ESTHER 6:14–7:10

VASHTI'S AND ESTHER'S EXPERIENCES IN THE GARDEN OF AHASUERUS

Vashti	Esther
Vashti's words are not recorded. She is silent in the text, and she sent her message to the king through the eunuchs.	Esther appealed directly to the king. Esther's trust in God demonstrated what God intends for relationships. Even the pagan king moved into right relationship when reacting to his wife's advocacy for her people.
Vashti hosted a banquet at the same time the king hosted a banquet.	Esther hosted a banquet, and the king attended.
The king demanded Vashti appear before his drunken friends.	The king invited Esther to make her requests.
Vashti tried to preserve her own dignity but lost her royal status.	Esther tried to preserve her own life and the lives of all the Jewish people at the risk of losing her life.
The king was partying in the garden.	The king was blowing off steam in the garden.
The anger of the king increased.	The anger of the king was abated.

11. What do we learn from these contrasting garden interactions about God's intent for flourishing relationships?

Early Christians familiar with the Old Testament would have recognized the backdrop of the palace garden as a familiar scene, and so should we. And I'll take it one step further: As modern readers, who know about King Jesus and the Garden of Gethsemane, I believe the Lord wants us to read Vashti's and Esther's garden stories in light of Jesus' garden story.

In the next lesson, we're going to explore what Jesus went through in the Garden of Gethsemane, and we are going to see echoes of Esther's experience in Esther 7. Again, we will have the main character facing a life-threatening decision to save their people. Esther, like Jesus, made her appeal to the king in a garden. The difference is that Esther maintained her position as queen and went down in Jewish history as a heroine; Jesus suffered crucifixion and went down in world history as the hero of all people.

✿ ✿ ✿

Let's check back in on our Gardens Storyline.

THE GARDENS STORYLINE OF SCRIPTURE

Location	Scripture(s)	The Presence of God
The Garden of Eden	Genesis 1–3	God walked with Adam and Eve in the Garden of Eden.
The Garden of Ahasuerus	Esther 1, 7	God was working behind the scenes to save his people.
The Garden of Gethsemane	Matthew 26	Christ agonized over his impending crucifixion.
The Gardens of the Crucifixion and Resurrection	John 19–20	Christ appeared to Mary Magdalene and commissioned her to tell the other disciples of his resurrection.
The Garden City	Revelation 21–22	God will come to dwell with his people.

The Protection of God	The Provision of God	The Produce of God
God did not let Adam and Eve live forever in a fallen world.	God provided substitutionary atonement.	God planted the Tree of Life.
God did not let Haman's plan come to fruition.	God gave Esther and Mordecai courage.	God planted Esther in the Garden of Ahasuerus so she could ask the king to save the Jewish people.
God does not require us to die as a consequence of our sin, because Jesus willingly gave his life to save ours.	Christ gave Christians his life.	Jesus is the Vine, and we are the branches.
Christ paid the penalty for our sins on the cross.	Christ rose from the dead, securing our future resurrection.	Jesus' resurrection foreshadows the resurrection of all believers in Christ.
God will wipe away all the tears from our eyes.	God will make all things new.	God will plant a new Garden City.

1. **What about this story in the Garden of Ahasuerus resonates with you most? What part of the story piques your curiosity?**

2. **What did you learn about God in this lesson? And what did you learn about yourself in this lesson?**

3. **How should these truths shape your faith community and change you?**

PART 4

RESPONDING

The purpose of Bible study is to help you become more Christlike; that's why part 4 will include journaling space for your reflection on and responses to the content and a blank checklist for actionable next steps. You'll be able to process what you're learning so that you can live out the concepts and pursue Christlikeness. Part 4 will enable you to answer the questions *What truths is this passage teaching?* and *How do I apply this to my life?*

ONE THING IS CLEAR: King Ahasuerus was not flourishing as God intends all people to flourish. He was in his garden, flaunting his material wealth and treating his wife like a prized possession. Instead of acting like an honorable king worthy of respect, coruling with his beloved, his presence in the garden was as menacing as the serpent's in the Garden of Eden. He was a king with no accountability and no boundaries.

A lot of Bible interpreters' conversations about the book of Esther discuss the so-called absence of God in the book, but I don't buy it. Just because he's not mentioned doesn't make God absent. As we read about the realities of a life planted away from him and the restoration and flourishing that happen when a person chooses to trust him, the entire story becomes a demonstration of God's unnoticed presence in our lives as the King we've always needed.

Relational brokenness, image bearers harming image bearers, is all around us. As I write this lesson, the sexual exploitation of innocent men and women is all over the news. Choose any industry, look up any news outlet, and there you'll find it: a story about a cover-up. A tale as old as King Ahasuerus's about wicked, powerful people mistreating the people in their care for their personal gain.

God is not recorded saying anything in the book of Esther, and I'm convinced that's because he already said everything he needed to on this matter in the Garden of Eden. We already know what is good, not good, and very good. God already told us what he thinks about the value and dignity of men and women. He already proved his trustworthiness and seriousness on these issues. The book of Esther shows us what happens to our relationships with God and our relationships with one another when we aren't acting out of trust and reliance on him.

This leads me to my reflections on this reading of Esther 1 and 7. I hope these points speak to you.

1. WE SERVE A GOOD KING.

This is basic, but it needs to be said: We serve a good King. Even though we know it to be true, it is one thing to know something and quite another to believe it and live it. You serve King Jesus. There is no one like him; none. In fact, I'd argue that—besides Christ—the world has never seen a truly good king. Some have had their moments, but none are honorable and worthy kings who rule unending kingdoms with righteousness and justice, peace and love. Sometimes the failures of leadership saturating the headlines tempt us to believe that there's no one we can really count on, no one we can really trust. But we can trust King Jesus. He's in the garden with us—advocating for us, protecting us, saving us.

2. GOOD KINGS DON'T EXPLOIT WOMEN.

King Jesus never exploited women. Instead, he healed women, talked to women, entrusted women with the gospel message, recruited female disciples, traveled with women, received financial support from women, applauded the faith of female disciples, and commissioned women for great-commission work. The longer I know him, the more I love him. Jesus is our good King, and he'd never treat men or women the way King Ahasuerus treated Vashti and Esther. He doesn't treat women (or men) like property or commodities. He doesn't objectify women (or men). He doesn't force women (or men) into following him or obeying him. He loves them. One of the many reasons Christ is a trustworthy King is that he provides safety and goodness in our relationship with him.

Use this journaling space to process what you are learning.

Ask yourself how these truths impact your relationship with God and with others.

What is the Holy Spirit bringing to your mind as actionable next steps in your faith journey?

- ✿
- ✿
- ✿

LESSON THREE

TRUSTING CHRIST'S SACRIFICE

THE GARDEN OF GETHSEMANE: THE SAVIOR'S GARDEN OF GRIEF

SCRIPTURE: MATTHEW 26

PART 1

CONTEXT

Before you begin your study, we will start with the context of the story we are about to read together: the setting, both cultural and historical; the people involved; and where our passage fits in the larger setting of Scripture. All these things help us make sense of what we're reading. Understanding the context of a Bible story is fundamental to reading Scripture well. Getting your bearings before you read will enable you to answer the question *What am I about to read?*

TAYLOR SWIFT FANS want her crowned queen of America. And that's the closest Americans are going to get to some type of monarchy. But we love to glamorize "the royals," whether they carry a scepter or not. Books about Queen Elizabeth, Princess Diana, and their children are regularly atop publishing best-seller lists. *The Crown* was a wildly popular show. We're obsessed with consuming content about royalty's every move.

In Bible times, royal dynasties were a topic of interest too. People in the ancient world clamored to have kings and queens. Even though God warned his people that a monarch would turn out to be unjust and oppressive, they still begged for a king, and he granted their request. This is the backdrop against which Matthew, the former tax collector turned Gospel writer, sets his historical narrative.

Matthew is on a mission: He is going to prove that Jesus is King.

Matthew opens his Gospel account with a lineage tracing the royalty of Israel and Jesus' connection to all the "greats" in the Old Testament. Jesus' human family tree confirms his kingship.

In Matthew's Gospel, Jesus is the new Moses on the new mountain with the new law leading the new Exodus for a new Passover. But he's also the long-awaited Jewish King and Messiah. Jesus isn't born in a palace, but the whole earth is his kingdom. His coronation is with a crown of thorns. He doesn't rule with might or threats, but his power is unrivaled.

He's unlike any king the world has ever seen or will ever see.

So far in our study we have seen kings in gardens—trustworthy and untrustworthy, ruling for good or reigning selfishly. Like God in the Garden of Eden and King Ahasuerus in the palace garden, Jesus comes to the Garden of Gethsemane to be with his people.

- God looked at his garden with delight.
- King Ahasuerus sat in his garden with anger.
- Jesus prayed in this garden with agony.

The Gospel of Matthew is often broken down into five sections, and we're going to be looking at the final section of the book, which is focused on "the passion of the Christ," or the events leading up to Jesus' crucifixion and resurrection. We are in the climax of the story.

Up until this point, Jesus has proven that he is not only the King of the world but also the kind of king who heals the sick, overpowers evil forces, and deputizes disciples to join his mission. He's the greatest leader of all time, but his leadership methods stand in contrast to expected methods of influence, both then and today. His leadership culminates in a self-sacrificing death and a miraculous resurrection.

Maybe, like me, you'll forget that Jesus is human in all this. He is 100 percent God, no doubt. But he is also 100 percent human. We tend to make similar

> The scene of Jesus's agonizing prayer is set in Gethsemane, traditionally thought to be a garden on the Mount of Olives (specifically, an olive grove if based on its etymology—"wine press"). That Matthew has not often presented Jesus in private prayer makes his cries to God in Gethsemane all the more poignant.[1]
>
> Jeannine K. Brown and Kyle Roberts, *Matthew*

mistakes when we think about our cultural royalty, princes and pop stars alike. If we're not careful, we can idolize celebrities and commodify their humanness for our own entertainment. As we read the Garden of Gethsemane story, it's vital that we remember that Jesus is fully God *and* fully human.

What you're about to read is a story about Jesus having something like a panic attack. He's processing his impending crucifixion and hoping that his closest friends will be by his side as he asks God to find another way to redemption. The narrative pulls you close so that you can almost feel Jesus breaking down.

This is a story about the kinds of friendships that fail us, the loneliness of being ghosted, the betrayal of abandonment, and the willingness of Jesus to suffer and die on our behalf. And where does God choose to host this moment in history? A garden. This is the return to the garden we've been waiting for: where a good King walks among the trees, demonstrating his trustworthiness as he moves to rescue us from our own rebellion and restore our relationship with him. The cost is high. In this garden, the soil is bloody and tear soaked. This is a King who embodies self-sacrifice. This is a King who loves you.

A lot of us feel like we're living in that antigarden, the barren ground of sin and the impossibility of making things right, whatever that means. As soon as we try to better ourselves, our relationships, our behavior, we find ourselves back in the cycle of sin and brokenness. What we find in the Garden of Gethsemane is a good King willing to die to bring the gardens of our souls back to life.

1. **PERSONAL CONTEXT: What is going on in your life right now that might impact how you understand the Garden of Gethsemane story? What do you hope to learn from this lesson?**

2. **SPIRITUAL CONTEXT: If you've never studied the Garden of Gethsemane before, what piques your curiosity? If you've studied this place before, what impressions and insights do you recall?**

3. **BIBLICAL CONTEXT: What questions come to mind as you read about the context of Jesus' surrender to the Cross or the Garden of Gethsemane? What questions do you wish you could have answered before studying this part of Scripture?**

PART 2

SEEING

Seeing the text is vital if we want the heart of the Scripture passage to sink in. We read slowly and intentionally through the text with the context in mind. As we practice close, thoughtful reading of Scripture, we pick up on phrases, implications, and meanings we might otherwise have missed. Part 2 includes close Scripture reading and observation questions to empower you to answer the question *What is the story saying?*

1. **Read Matthew 26:1-56. Underline any locations mentioned in the chapter and draw a box around the places Jesus goes.**

26 When Jesus had finished saying all these things, he said to his
disciples, 2 "You know that after two days the Passover is coming, and the
Son of Man will be handed over to be crucified."
3 Then the chief priests and the elders of the people gathered in the
palace of the high priest, who was called Caiaphas, 4 and they conspired
to arrest Jesus by stealth and kill him. 5 But they said, "Not during the
festival, or there may be a riot among the people."
6 Now while Jesus was at Bethany in the house of Simon the leper, 7 a
woman came to him with an alabaster jar of very costly ointment, and she
poured it on his head as he sat at the table. 8 But when the disciples saw

it, they were angry and said, “Why this waste? 9 For this ointment could
have been sold for a large sum, and the money given to the poor.” 10 But
Jesus, aware of this, said to them, “Why do you trouble the woman? She
has performed a good service for me. 11 For you always have the poor with
you, but you will not always have me. 12 By pouring this ointment on my
body she has prepared me for burial. 13 Truly I tell you, wherever this good
news is proclaimed in the whole world, what she has done will be told in
remembrance of her.”

14 Then one of the twelve, who was called Judas Iscariot, went to the
chief priests 15 and said, “What will you give me if I betray him to you?”
They paid him thirty pieces of silver. 16 And from that moment he began to
look for an opportunity to betray him.

17 On the first day of Unleavened Bread the disciples came to Jesus,
saying, “Where do you want us to make the preparations for you to eat
the Passover?” 18 He said, “Go into the city to a certain man, and say to
him, ‘The Teacher says, My time is near; I will keep the Passover at your
house with my disciples.’” 19 So the disciples did as Jesus had directed
them, and they prepared the Passover meal.

20 When it was evening, he took his place with the twelve; 21 and while
they were eating, he said, “Truly I tell you, one of you will betray me.”
22 And they became greatly distressed and began to say to him one after
another, “Surely not I, Lord?” 23 He answered, “The one who has dipped
his hand into the bowl with me will betray me. 24 The Son of Man goes
as it is written of him, but woe to that one by whom the Son of Man is
betrayed! It would have been better for that one not to have been born.”
25 Judas, who betrayed him, said, “Surely not I, Rabbi?” He replied, “You
have said so.”

26 While they were eating, Jesus took a loaf of bread, and after
blessing it he broke it, gave it to the disciples, and said, “Take, eat; this
is my body.” 27 Then he took a cup, and after giving thanks he gave it
to them, saying, “Drink from it, all of you; 28 for this is my blood of the

covenant, which is poured out for many for the forgiveness of sins. 29 I tell
you, I will never again drink of this fruit of the vine until that day when I
drink it new with you in my Father's kingdom."
30 When they had sung the hymn, they went out to the Mount of Olives.
31 Then Jesus said to them, "You will all become deserters because of
me this night; for it is written,

'I will strike the shepherd,
and the sheep of the flock will be scattered.'

32 But after I am raised up, I will go ahead of you to Galilee." 33 Peter said
to him, "Though all become deserters because of you, I will never desert
you." 34 Jesus said to him, "Truly I tell you, this very night, before the cock
crows, you will deny me three times." 35 Peter said to him, "Even though I
must die with you, I will not deny you." And so said all the disciples.
36 Then Jesus went with them to a place called Gethsemane; and he
said to his disciples, "Sit here while I go over there and pray." 37 He took
with him Peter and the two sons of Zebedee, and began to be grieved and
agitated. 38 Then he said to them, "I am deeply grieved, even to death;
remain here, and stay awake with me." 39 And going a little farther, he
threw himself on the ground and prayed, "My Father, if it is possible, let
this cup pass from me; yet not what I want but what you want." 40 Then he
came to the disciples and found them sleeping; and he said to Peter, "So,
could you not stay awake with me one hour? 41 Stay awake and pray that
you may not come into the time of trial; the spirit indeed is willing, but the
flesh is weak." 42 Again he went away for the second time and prayed, "My
Father, if this cannot pass unless I drink it, your will be done." 43 Again he
came and found them sleeping, for their eyes were heavy. 44 So leaving
them again, he went away and prayed for the third time, saying the same
words. 45 Then he came to the disciples and said to them, "Are you still
sleeping and taking your rest? See, the hour is at hand, and the Son of

Man is betrayed into the hands of sinners. 46 Get up, let us be going. See,
my betrayer is at hand."
47 While he was still speaking, Judas, one of the twelve, arrived; with
him was a large crowd with swords and clubs, from the chief priests
and the elders of the people. 48 Now the betrayer had given them a sign,
saying, "The one I will kiss is the man; arrest him." 49 At once he came up to
Jesus and said, "Greetings, Rabbi!" and kissed him. 50 Jesus said to him,
"Friend, do what you are here to do." Then they came and laid hands on
Jesus and arrested him. 51 Suddenly, one of those with Jesus put his hand
on his sword, drew it, and struck the slave of the high priest, cutting off his
ear. 52 Then Jesus said to him, "Put your sword back into its place; for all
who take the sword will perish by the sword. 53 Do you think that I cannot
appeal to my Father, and he will at once send me more than twelve
legions of angels? 54 But how then would the scriptures be fulfilled, which
say it must happen in this way?" 55 At that hour Jesus said to the crowds,
"Have you come out with swords and clubs to arrest me as though I were
a bandit? Day after day I sat in the temple teaching, and you did not
arrest me. 56 But all this has taken place, so that the scriptures of the
prophets may be fulfilled." Then all the disciples deserted him and fled.

MATTHEW 26:1-56

2. **Why do you think Jesus went to the Garden of Gethsemane to pray? Why do you think Judas went to the Garden of Gethsemane to betray Jesus?**

- **Jesus:**

- **Judas:**

3. If you were Jesus, what would you be thinking in the Garden of Gethsemane? What range of emotions would you feel? List anything that comes to mind.

4. If you were Peter, James, or John, the three disciples invited to pray with Jesus and be with him in his time of greatest need, how would you have processed the Garden of Gethsemane events? List anything that comes to mind.

5. What unanswered questions do you have about the Garden of Gethsemane or anything else you've read so far?

Jesus' faithfulness in seeking and following God's direction stands in contrast with the frailty of his disciples. They fail to keep watch (see chs. 24–25) and do not pray, as Jesus had instructed ([26:41] and 6:13), to be delivered from the test (*peirasmos*)—both the present crisis and the eschatological trial.[2]

Barbara E. Reid, *The Gospel according to Matthew*

6. What encouraged you most in your reading?

Agitated Jesus can be disconcerting. We often picture Jesus as calm and collected (except for that one time he flipped over tables in righteous anger). But Jesus is fully God and fully human. He has experienced the full range of human emotions—including distress, panic, and agitation.

PART 3

UNDERSTANDING

Now that we've finished a close reading of the Scriptures, we're going to spend some time on interpretation: doing our best to understand what God was saying to the original audience and what he's teaching us through the process. But to do so, we need to learn his ways and consider how God's Word would have been understood by the original audience before applying the same truths to our own lives. "Scripture interpretation" may sound a little stuffy, but understanding what God means to communicate to us in the Bible is crucial to enjoying a close relationship with Jesus. Part 3 will enable you to answer the question *What does it mean?*

WE ALL HAVE GETHSEMANES, those places in our stories where agony defines the environment. Yes, Gethsemane was a real place; historical moments did happen there—but this garden also represents the human experience. Gethsemane is not just the garden in which Jesus wept or the place where the disciples deserted their Lord, one of their best friends. This geographical location symbolizes pain points in the lives of the Jewish people and in our own spiritual journeys, places where we can choose to trust that God's ways are leading to our ultimate flourishing.

For some of our nearest and dearest, Gethsemane is infertility, losing a parent or child, or leaving a church wounded. Your Gethsemane might be job loss, a broken relationship, or an extended season of loneliness. But what unites our experiences is this: The presence of suffering is unavoidable if you're human. Unless we are willing to accompany Jesus into the Garden of Gethsemane—willing to trust that our pain and sorrow are not only welcome but deeply understood—we are just like the tired disciples, whose sleep kept them at arm's length from the shared grief before them.

In ancient times, readers of Matthew 26 may have recognized the familiar setting for the story, a garden, and connected it to the other important gardens in the Old Testament. Their Jewish imagination could have linked the temptation in the Garden of Eden to the deposition in the Garden of Ahasuerus and to the betrayal in the Garden of Gethsemane. In some ways, the three gardens repeat a tale as old as time: Humans sin. But thanks be to God, that's not the whole story.

Gardens in the Bible are not just about human failure. They are also about Christ's victory.

1. Read this paraphrase of Matthew 26:36-56 (MSG) and circle anything Jesus says.

> **36-38 Then Jesus went with them to a garden called Gethsemane and told his disciples, "Stay here while I go over there and pray." Taking along Peter and the two sons of Zebedee, he plunged into an agonizing sorrow. Then he said, "This sorrow is crushing my life out. Stay here and keep vigil with me."**
>
> **39 Going a little ahead, he fell on his face, praying, "My Father, if there is any way, get me out of this. But please, not what I want. You, what do *you* want?"**
>
> **40-41 When he came back to his disciples, he found them sound asleep. He said to Peter, "Can't you stick it out with me a single hour? Stay alert; be in prayer so you don't wander into temptation without even knowing you're in danger. There is a part of you that is eager, ready for anything in God. But there's another part that's as lazy as an old dog sleeping by the fire."**

42 He then left them a second time. Again he prayed, "My Father, if
there is no other way than this, drinking this cup to the dregs, I'm ready.
Do it your way."

43-44 When he came back, he again found them sound asleep. They
simply couldn't keep their eyes open. This time he let them sleep on, and
went back a third time to pray, going over the same ground one last time.

45-46 When he came back the next time, he said, "Are you going to sleep
on and make a night of it? My time is up, the Son of Man is about to be
handed over to the hands of sinners. Get up! Let's get going! My betrayer
is here."

47-49 The words were barely out of his mouth when Judas (the one from
the Twelve) showed up, and with him a gang from the high priests and
religious leaders brandishing swords and clubs. The betrayer had worked
out a sign with them: "The one I kiss, that's the one—seize him." He went
straight to Jesus, greeted him, "How are you, Rabbi?" and kissed him.

50-51 Jesus said, "Friend, why this charade?"

Then they came on him—grabbed him and roughed him up. One of
those with Jesus pulled his sword and, taking a swing at the Chief Priest's
servant, cut off his ear.

52-54 Jesus said, "Put your sword back where it belongs. All who use
swords are destroyed by swords. Don't you realize that I am able right
now to call to my Father, and twelve companies—more, if I want them—of
fighting angels would be here, battle-ready? But if I did that, how would
the Scriptures come true that say this is the way it has to be?"

55-56 Then Jesus addressed the mob: "What is this—coming out after
me with swords and clubs as if I were a dangerous criminal? Day after
day I have been sitting in the Temple teaching, and you never so much as
lifted a hand against me. You've done it this way to confirm and fulfill the
prophetic writings."

Then all the disciples cut and ran.

MATTHEW 26:36-56, MSG

2. Which of the words of Jesus stand out to you most and why?

I can't believe Jesus took Peter, James, and John with him to Gethsemane knowing they would fall asleep during his most tender moments of ministry. Or that he returned to them three times, even as he suffered extreme grief, to challenge them, to invite them to be with him in the pain—which they would soon experience as well. What patience, what mercy. Jesus could have struck them dead or cursed their behavior.

I can't believe Jesus went to Gethsemane knowing that's where Judas would turn him over to the people who wanted him dead. He journeyed to his favorite prayer spot, a place he'd come often with his disciples, a safe place to commune with God, only to have that sacred space become a battlefield.

3. Have you ever experienced wounds from a friend? How did that experience impact your faith in God and your relationships with others?

4. What's your Garden of Gethsemane? Metaphorically speaking, where in your life have you experienced agony, and how has Jesus' presence ministered to you there?

My Garden of Gethsemane was the ICU at Baylor Hospital Dallas,[3] where my dad suffered for two weeks before he passed. If not for the presence of Christ, I never would have made it through those weeks of agony.

The Garden of Gethsemane was supposed to be a place of delight but was now a place of agony. I hate that Jesus went through the Garden of Gethsemane, that all of us have metaphorical places in our lives that we might term Gethsemanes. But I'm also thankful that Jesus didn't bypass this garden. He went through it for us. If we ever wonder if he's really in it with us, this moment in his life proves his solidarity with us to the bitter end. In addition to being the suffering Savior and the victorious Christ, he is also the grieving Savior who knows how to comfort us when we experience grief.

When everyone around us can't hold vigil during our suffering, King Jesus abides. He tends to our every need and rushes to the side of the brokenhearted. When it feels like our circumstances are crushing the life out of us, King Jesus can say, *I understand.* And he will mean it. He did all this for us. For you. He endured betrayal, humiliation, abuse, abandonment, and crushing loss to be our suffering servant, the true King of kings and Lord of lords.

We serve a God who walks beside us in our gardens with his faithful presence, tender mercy, and constant companionship. He intercedes for us even now as we read, underline, and study. No matter how long you must remain in your personal Garden of Gethsemane, you can be there as long as Jesus is with you.

And he is.

5. **How do you think first-century Christians would have interpreted the Garden of Gethsemane story?**

MAKING CONNECTIONS

An important part of understanding the meaning of a Bible passage is getting a sense of its place in the broader storyline of Scripture. When we make connections between different parts of the Bible, we get a glimpse of the unity and cohesion of the Scriptures.

Recently I went with my husband, Aaron, to watch U2 perform at the Sphere in Las Vegas. It was epic, y'all. As I have declared before, U2 is the greatest rock band of all time. Facts. End of story. It kills me that there is a whole generation of music lovers who've never heard Bono's songs. He sings songs of lament for those of us who still haven't found what we're looking for, who are stuck in a moment and unable to get out of it, who are longing for a world where we carry each other because love is all we have left.

6. **Lament is the expression of grief or pain. On a scale from 1 to 10 (with 1 meaning "not at all" and 10 meaning "completely comfortable"), how comfortable are you with lament? Why do you think that is the case?**

1 2 3 4 5 6 7 8 9 10

God's people lament throughout Scripture. And for generations, in moments of terror, anguish, anxiety, and longing, Jewish people sang Psalm 42 as a desperate plea for God's help. It should be no surprise to us, then, that as Jesus wrestled with the reality of the Cross and the agony of his sacrificial death, he did so by repeating that ancient song.

7. Read Psalm 42. Underline each question and put a box around verse 5.

42 As a deer longs for flowing streams,
  so my soul longs for you, O God.
2 My soul thirsts for God,
  for the living God.
When shall I come and behold
  the face of God?
3 My tears have been my food
  day and night,
while people say to me continually,
  "Where is your God?"

4 These things I remember,
  as I pour out my soul:
how I went with the throng,
  and led them in procession to the house of God,
with glad shouts and songs of thanksgiving,
  a multitude keeping festival.
5 Why are you cast down, O my soul,
  and why are you disquieted within me?
Hope in God; for I shall again praise him,
  my help 6 and my God.

My soul is cast down within me;
  therefore I remember you

from the land of Jordan and of Hermon,
  from Mount Mizar.
7 Deep calls to deep
  at the thunder of your cataracts;
all your waves and your billows
  have gone over me.
8 By day the LORD commands his steadfast love,
  and at night his song is with me,
  a prayer to the God of my life.

9 I say to God, my rock,
  "Why have you forgotten me?
Why must I walk about mournfully
  because the enemy oppresses me?"
10 As with a deadly wound in my body,
  my adversaries taunt me,
while they say to me continually,
  "Where is your God?"

11 Why are you cast down, O my soul,
  and why are you disquieted within me?
Hope in God; for I shall again praise him,
  my help and my God.

PSALM 42

In Matthew 26:38, Jesus seems to have Psalm 42:5 in the background.[4] His soul is downcast, overwhelmed, grieved to the point of death.

Don't miss this. Jesus was so overcome with distress that he grieved in a way that made him feel like he was dying. Some of us know that feeling well. We know what it is to stare down depression and want it all to end, what it's like to feel physical pain because the trauma feels like it is in our bones. You and I know what it is to feel oppressed, depressed, disquieted, mournful, forgotten, and downcast. And so does Jesus. In fact, he entered the pain to experience everything we've been through and will go through. He is the man of sorrows, the suffering servant willing to endure the consequences of our sin and the hardships we live through.

8. **Jesus—fully human, but also fully God—knew this whole psalm. What other questions in this psalm resonate with you? When you think about Jesus reflecting on these questions in a very personal way, which ones surprise you?**

9. **The second part of verse 5 speaks of hope in God. How does it make you feel to know that God himself, even knowing he is the ultimate hope and helper, experienced this kind of hopelessness and grief?**

10. Which Bible verses are your go-to Scriptures when you are suffering? Write them out below.

Jesus experienced the most painful suffering a human can go through—and he did this because he loves us unconditionally. Your circumstances are no match for his unstoppable love for you. There is no weakness in crying out to God for help, no shame in bearing the weight of the world's brokenness in tears and lament. Jesus did the same thing.

You have permission to be sad about sin's impact on our world and in your life. Also: We are not meant to stay in the Garden of Gethsemane. God walked through a garden of pain and death so he could bring us back to life. We are not fated to suffer; that's not how our story ends. Like Jesus, we will move on from Gethsemane to the Garden of Resurrection.

✿ ✿ ✿

Let's check back in on our Gardens Storyline.

THE GARDENS STORYLINE OF SCRIPTURE

Location	Scripture(s)	The Presence of God
The Garden of Eden	Genesis 1–3	God walked with Adam and Eve in the Garden of Eden.
The Garden of Ahasuerus	Esther 1, 7	God was working behind the scenes to save his people.
The Garden of Gethsemane	Matthew 26	Christ agonized over his impending crucifixion.
The Gardens of the Crucifixion and Resurrection	John 19–20	Christ appeared to Mary Magdalene and commissioned her to tell the other disciples of his resurrection.
The Garden City	Revelation 21–22	God will come to dwell with his people.

The Protection of God	The Provision of God	The Produce of God
God did not let Adam and Eve live forever in a fallen world.	God provided substitutionary atonement.	God planted the Tree of Life.
God did not let Haman's plan come to fruition.	God gave Esther and Mordecai courage.	God planted Esther in the Garden of Ahasuerus so she could ask the king to save the Jewish people.
God does not require us to die as a consequence of our sin, because Jesus willingly gave his life to save ours.	Christ gave Christians his life.	Jesus is the Vine, and we are the branches.
Christ paid the penalty for our sins on the cross.	Christ rose from the dead, securing our future resurrection.	Jesus' resurrection foreshadows the resurrection of all believers in Christ.
God will wipe away all the tears from our eyes.	God will make all things new.	God will plant a new Garden City.

1. **What about the Garden of Gethsemane story resonates with you most? What part of the story piques your curiosity?**

2. **What did you learn about God in this lesson? And what did you learn about yourself in this lesson?**

3. **How should these truths shape your faith community and change you?**

PART 4

RESPONDING

The purpose of Bible study is to help you become more Christlike; that's why part 4 will include journaling space for your reflection on and responses to the content and a blank checklist for actionable next steps. You'll be able to process what you're learning so that you can live out the concepts and pursue Christlikeness. Part 4 will enable you to answer the questions *What truths is this passage teaching?* and *How do I apply this to my life?*

JUST A YEAR after my father's tragic death by suicide, I visited the Holy Land. It was no secret to my travel companions that I was mournful on the trip. I often secluded myself at the back of the bus to hide my tears.

And so I brought my own heartbreak to the place of Jesus' anguish, a garden full of olive trees traditionally known as the Garden of Gethsemane. We had a divine appointment in that garden together, me and Jesus. Because Jesus wept in that same garden, I let him wipe my tears there too.

I'd known that the Garden of Gethsemane was on the side of the Mount of Olives, but only when I put my feet in the dirt at Gethsemane, looking around to take in the view of the mountainside, was I able to gain a new perspective. Looking up and out from the garden, you can see breathtaking views of Jerusalem and what remains of the Temple—a reminder that Jesus is King and rules and reigns even now over evil forces and the brokenness of the world.

My Garden of Gethsemane experience was full of anguish but also full of hope.

We should not bypass our feelings or ignore the hard work required to process through grief. But neither are we left alone. Instead, we are invited to walk with Jesus in our gardens of agony. He's familiar with those places, after all. And he's lived through them in victory. My dad's death was not the end of his story or mine. Because Jesus entered the pain of the world, I know the deeper truths about the garden of grief.

I'm ready to move on from the Garden of Gethsemane because I'm at about a 4 out of 10 when it comes to lament. Before we do, let's reflect on the deeper truths in this garden scene.

1. JESUS NEVER DESERTS YOU.

In the Garden of Eden, Jesus was present. He suffered as he watched Adam and Eve's exile from paradise. In the Garden of Ahasuerus, Jesus was present. He suffered as he watched the banishment of Queen Vashti and the threat against the people of God. And in the Garden of Gethsemane, Jesus was present while he suffered through the pain of abandonment. Point being: Jesus was there the whole time. And this becomes the mantra of Christians who live through hard things: *He was there the whole time.* Even though Jesus' closest friends and ministry partners deserted him during his time of greatest need, he has not done that with us, nor will he do so. When I grieve, I say things to God like *Where were you?*

Jesus was left utterly alone, humanly speaking. In spite of his efforts to warn them about his coming rejection and suffering, the disciples were not ready for this turn of events. . . . It must have been very painful for Jesus to be abandoned by his hand-picked disciples. This abandonment was part of the price he was called upon to pay as he sought to bring in the kingdom of God through his life and ministry.[5]

Brian Wintle, "Matthew," in *South Asia Bible Commentary*

How could you? This is normal. Healthy, even. But after some time, we all come to realize that Jesus never left us. He was with us through it all.

To everyone who feels isolated by sorrow, remember this: Jesus never deserts you. Everyone else you count on might tuck tail and scatter when it gets hard, but Jesus won't. When you think your hardships have stolen everything good you ever had or will ever have, Jesus remains faithful, ever present, near to your broken heart.

2. JESUS MOVED ON FROM THE GARDEN OF GETHSEMANE, AND SO CAN YOU.

Do you know how Jesus moved on from the Garden of Gethsemane? By Roman escort. Judas betrayed Jesus with a kiss—next-level and pitiful deception on Judas's part—and sent Jesus on to his trials and eventually to his death. The next garden God would walk in was the Garden of the Crucifixion.

But after death is resurrection. Jesus got out of Gethsemane, and so will we. If Gethsemane represents the gut-wrenching parts of our story, this needs to be said: You can move on from this tear-soaked garden because Jesus did. *Get us out of here, Jesus, and take us to the Garden of Resurrection.* To quote Bono, "[We] go there with you, it's all [we] can do."[6] Jesus is going to get us out of our Gethsemanes. Praise God that there are more gardens in the Bible!

Use this journaling space to process what you are learning.

Ask yourself how these truths impact your relationship with God and with others.

What is the Holy Spirit bringing to your mind as actionable next steps in your faith journey?

- ✿
- ✿
- ✿

LESSON FOUR

TRUSTING CHRIST'S RESURRECTION

THE GARDENS OF THE CRUCIFIXION AND RESURRECTION: THE COSMIC GARDENER RISES FROM THE DEAD

SCRIPTURE: JOHN 19–20

PART 1

CONTEXT

Before you begin your study, we will start with the context of the story we are about to read together: the setting, both cultural and historical; the people involved; and where our passage fits in the larger setting of Scripture. All these things help us make sense of what we're reading. Understanding the context of a Bible story is fundamental to reading Scripture well. Getting your bearings before you read will enable you to answer the question *What am I about to read?*

MY SON, CALEB, is obsessed with car-racing video games. Because fancy sports cars. His favorite video-game feature is the Rewind button, to throw a car in reverse to an exact point in history so that he can steer his Lamborghini in a new direction. Car crashes, running into ditches, and flipping cars end over end don't cause Caleb any fear because he knows he can move his finger and, voilà, good as new.

Wouldn't it be amazing if we could maneuver similarly in our personal lives? What if we could reverse self-sabotage, nasty habits, sticky relationships, and family rifts? Wouldn't it be wonderful to touch a button, throw our lives back to a certain point in time, and start again fresh? I wish that existed. There's no Easy Button for life, no reverse lever we can pull.

But Jesus does give us an epic redo on a cosmic level through his life, death, and resurrection.

Jesus, the Savior of the world. He offers you and me a total reversal.

- We don't have to be the perpetual screw-ups, the chronically unmotivated, the always unlucky in love; Jesus, who died to give us new life, secured us role reversals.
- We won't always mourn lost time, lost opportunities, lost dreams; Jesus, who is not bound by time, gives us hope that time lost will be made new.

You and I, we're people of resurrection. God replants our lives, restores our trust, reignites our passions, and recovers what feels beyond hope.

In this lesson, we're going to explore the ultimate cosmic redo, Christ's resurrection. In God's providence, this do-over happens in two different gardens. While these gardens were in different geographical locations, we are meant to look at them side by side; the two scenes are coupled intentionally in the Scriptures.

You don't get resurrection without death, and death is incomplete without the Resurrection.

Here's the good news: We're not stuck in our metaphorical gardens of grief, like Gethsemane. We are not abandoned to our gardens of death, like the Crucifixion. You and I get to move on, like Jesus did, into the Garden of Resurrection. Because he lives, we can face tomorrow.[1] His resurrection from the dead is a preview of our future. We, too, are going to rise from the dead after we die, like Jesus.

What you're about to read is a portion of John's Gospel, a storied history from the beloved disciple's perspective. The books of Matthew, Mark, and Luke are called the synoptic Gospels, and most of the stories they tell are shared among the three perspectives. But John's Gospel is unique. John makes sure to bring Jesus' deity front and center. John records more conversations and more of Jesus' words with people than the other Gospel accounts.

The Gospel of John starts with the first three words from Genesis: *In the beginning*. This is John's signal to us that his book is another creation story, another fresh start. Where Genesis is about our first beginning, the Gospel of John is about our *new* beginning. Whatever was lost in the Garden of Eden is reclaimed in the Gardens of the Crucifixion and Resurrection.

John is explicit about his goal: He wants his book to confirm our faith in Jesus, who is superior to any other so-called gods (John 20:31). Jesus is the one true God. He is the Savior of the world. He's ruling as King over all the gardens of the earth, and he initiated his redemption the way he kicked it all off "in the beginning"—by visiting a garden and offering us everything we need for an epic redo.

The Resurrection miracle is that God comes back to life in a garden so we can come back to him in a garden.

At this point in our study, I hope you feel a bit of angst that the gardens we've looked at so far have not gone the way they should have. Adam and Eve should have chosen to trust the wisdom giver, to walk with him in the garden so they could learn what they needed for a fruitful life. King Ahasuerus should not have requested Queen Vashti leave her party to parade in front of drunken men or demeaned and destroyed his relationship with her. The disciples should have stayed awake in the Garden of Gethsemane, and Judas should not have betrayed Christ there either.

Humans mess things up. We have been created for paradise, for gardens where the King dwells with his people and where men and women enjoy each other's dignified presence as image bearers of God. But so far what we've found in the gardens in Scripture is a sin cycle: Humans have a way of turning paradise into a pit of despair. I believe the Lord authored the Scriptures this way so that we would feel longing in each story. A longing to return to Eden, yes—but even better, a vision of a new and better garden that won't ever be subject to the tyranny of sin and brokenness.

What I hope you notice in the text today is the unfailing love of Jesus. He just won't give up on us. Even if he has to go to his death, he will redeem all the gardens and all the garden dwellers. He really is the good Gardener.

A prime example of Jesus' power to redeem is John, the author of the passage we are going to study in this lesson. Even though he'd witnessed Jesus' miracles, participated in his earthly ministry, and lain as close to him as a child would to his father, John wasn't a perfect disciple. He doubted God's plan, fell asleep when

Jesus needed his friendship the most, and left the cross to hide in the Upper Room, plagued by fear.

But on the other side of the Resurrection, John helped start the early church. He healed the sick. His writing is part of God's inspired Word. God even gave him a vision of the end of time and the restoration of all things.

No matter how your life has gone so far, you are not fated for failure. You are not designed for destruction, and you are not a slave to some inevitable end. You were created to live—to live fully, fruitfully—and to begin again and again. You've got redos in your future because King Jesus is coming back again to live with us forever in a new garden.

1. **PERSONAL CONTEXT: What is going on in your life right now that might impact how you understand the Gardens of the Crucifixion and Resurrection? What do you hope to learn from this lesson?**

2. **SPIRITUAL CONTEXT: If you've never studied the Gardens of the Crucifixion and Resurrection before, what piques your curiosity? If you've studied these places before, what impressions and insights do you recall?**

3. **BIBLICAL CONTEXT: What questions come to mind as you read about the context of Jesus' crucifixion and resurrection? What questions do you wish you could have answered before studying this part of Scripture?**

PART 2

SEEING

Seeing the text is vital if we want the heart of the Scripture passage to sink in. We read slowly and intentionally through the text with the context in mind. As we practice close, thoughtful reading of Scripture, we pick up on phrases, implications, and meanings we might otherwise have missed. Part 2 includes close Scripture reading and observation questions to empower you to answer the question *What is the story saying?*

1. **Read John 19:14–20:18. Underline any mention of Scripture being fulfilled, and circle any reference to *cloth*, *wine*, *garden*, or *king*.**

**14 Now it was the day of Preparation for the Passover; and it was about
noon. [Pilate] said to the Jews, "Here is your King!" 15 They cried out,
"Away with him! Away with him! Crucify him!" Pilate asked them, "Shall I
crucify your King?" The chief priests answered, "We have no king but the
emperor." 16 Then he handed [Jesus] over to them to be crucified.**

**So they took Jesus; 17 and carrying the cross by himself, he went out to
what is called The Place of the Skull, which in Hebrew is called Golgotha.
18 There they crucified him, and with him two others, one on either side,
with Jesus between them. 19 Pilate also had an inscription written and
put on the cross. It read, "Jesus of Nazareth, the King of the Jews."**

[20] Many of the Jews read this inscription, because the place where Jesus
was crucified was near the city; and it was written in Hebrew, in Latin,
and in Greek. [21] Then the chief priests of the Jews said to Pilate, "Do not
write, 'The King of the Jews,' but, 'This man said, I am King of the Jews.'"
[22] Pilate answered, "What I have written I have written." [23] When the
soldiers had crucified Jesus, they took his clothes and divided them into
four parts, one for each soldier. They also took his tunic; now the tunic was
seamless, woven in one piece from the top. [24] So they said to one another,
"Let us not tear it, but cast lots for it to see who will get it." This was to
fulfill what the scripture says,

"They divided my clothes among themselves,
  and for my clothing they cast lots."

[25] And that is what the soldiers did.

Meanwhile, standing near the cross of Jesus were his mother, and his
mother's sister, Mary the wife of Clopas, and Mary Magdalene. [26] When
Jesus saw his mother and the disciple whom he loved standing beside her,
he said to his mother, "Woman, here is your son." [27] Then he said to the
disciple, "Here is your mother." And from that hour the disciple took her
into his own home.

[28] After this, when Jesus knew that all was now finished, he said (in
order to fulfill the scripture), "I am thirsty." [29] A jar full of sour wine was
standing there. So they put a sponge full of the wine on a branch of
hyssop and held it to his mouth. [30] When Jesus had received the wine, he
said, "It is finished." Then he bowed his head and gave up his spirit.

[31] Since it was the day of Preparation, the Jews did not want the
bodies left on the cross during the sabbath, especially because that
sabbath was a day of great solemnity. So they asked Pilate to have the
legs of the crucified men broken and the bodies removed. [32] Then the
soldiers came and broke the legs of the first and of the other who had

been crucified with him. 33 But when they came to Jesus and saw that he was already dead, they did not break his legs. 34 Instead, one of the soldiers pierced his side with a spear, and at once blood and water came out. 35 (He who saw this has testified so that you also may believe. His testimony is true, and he knows that he tells the truth.) 36 These things occurred so that the scripture might be fulfilled, "None of his bones shall be broken." 37 And again another passage of scripture says, "They will look on the one whom they have pierced."

38 After these things, Joseph of Arimathea, who was a disciple of Jesus, though a secret one because of his fear of the Jews, asked Pilate to let him take away the body of Jesus. Pilate gave him permission; so he came and removed his body. 39 Nicodemus, who had at first come to Jesus by night, also came, bringing a mixture of myrrh and aloes, weighing about a hundred pounds. 40 They took the body of Jesus and wrapped it with the spices in linen cloths, according to the burial custom of the Jews. 41 Now there was a garden in the place where he was crucified, and in the garden there was a new tomb in which no one had ever been laid. 42 And so, because it was the Jewish day of Preparation, and the tomb was nearby, they laid Jesus there.

20 Early on the first day of the week, while it was still dark, Mary Magdalene came to the tomb and saw that the stone had been removed from the tomb. 2 So she ran and went to Simon Peter and the other disciple, the one whom Jesus loved, and said to them, "They have taken the Lord out of the tomb, and we do not know where they have laid him." 3 Then Peter and the other disciple set out and went toward the tomb. 4 The two were running together, but the other disciple outran Peter and reached the tomb first. 5 He bent down to look in and saw the linen wrappings lying there, but he did not go in. 6 Then Simon Peter came, following him, and went into the tomb. He saw the linen wrappings lying there, 7 and the cloth that had been on Jesus' head, not lying with the linen wrappings but rolled up in a place by itself. 8 Then the other disciple,

who reached the tomb first, also went in, and he saw and believed; [9] for
as yet they did not understand the scripture, that he must rise from the
dead. [10] Then the disciples returned to their homes.

[11] But Mary stood weeping outside the tomb. As she wept, she bent
over to look into the tomb; [12] and she saw two angels in white, sitting
where the body of Jesus had been lying, one at the head and the other
at the feet. [13] They said to her, "Woman, why are you weeping?" She said
to them, "They have taken away my Lord, and I do not know where they
have laid him." [14] When she had said this, she turned around and saw
Jesus standing there, but she did not know that it was Jesus. [15] Jesus
said to her, "Woman, why are you weeping? Whom are you looking for?"
Supposing him to be the gardener, she said to him, "Sir, if you have
carried him away, tell me where you have laid him, and I will take him
away." [16] Jesus said to her, "Mary!" She turned and said to him in Hebrew,
"Rabbouni!" (which means Teacher). [17] Jesus said to her, "Do not hold
on to me, because I have not yet ascended to the Father. But go to my
brothers and say to them, 'I am ascending to my Father and your Father,
to my God and your God.'" [18] Mary Magdalene went and announced to the
disciples, "I have seen the Lord"; and she told them that he had said these
things to her.

JOHN 19:14–20:18

2. Write out what the chief priests say to Pilate about Jesus in John 19:15:

That any Jew, let alone a chief priest, would give allegiance to the Roman authorities is stunning. The Romans were their oppressors, people who followed pagan gods. The chief priests' words were politically expedient and a betrayal of their allegiance to Yahweh.

3. **In John's telling of this story, Jesus is carrying the cross by himself (John 19:17). But we know from other Gospels that someone eventually did help him carry the cross. Why do you think John intentionally left out this detail in his Gospel account?**

Jesus and the cross made it to Golgotha, "The Place of the Skull" (John 19:17). For the Jewish people watching, I wonder if the setting of this gruesome death triggered their memory of the prophet Ezekiel's vision of the valley of dry bones. Jesus would eventually echo Ezekiel's prophecy, rising from the dead: "I open your graves, and bring you up from your graves, O my people. I will put my spirit within you, and you shall live" (Ezekiel 37:13-14). He really does turn graves into gardens.

Something else that stands out to me in this reading is that in the Garden of Gethsemane Jesus was surrounded by people but alone. As he suffered, his friends, who were supposed to join him in prayer, were asleep. Now, as he suffered on the cross, he was again surrounded—this time by criminals. These men were with him to the very end.

4. Why were the Jews so upset with Pilate's cross inscription? And how did they want Pilate to edit the inscription? What difference would that have made?

First-century Roman culture was highly stratified by status. The people at the top were affluent, influential, and in leadership in the empire. The people at the bottom were enslaved. The Romans would use crucifixions to make a statement to criminals and the enslaved: Break the law, and you die a shameful death. Cross us, and you'll go to the cross. Calling Jesus the King of the Jews was meant to shame both Jesus and the Jewish people. Kings don't suffer a shameful slave death; they're supposed to reign supreme in power.

5. Whom did you expect to be at the foot of the cross while Jesus was being crucified? And who is noticeably absent?

6. **Write out the first three words of Genesis and John and then write out John 19:30 to the right of them. Below the phrases, write any reflections that come to mind.**

   - **First three words of Genesis:**

   - **First three words of John:**

7. **Based on John 19:38, what kind of disciple was Joseph of Arimathea?**

I am both comforted and challenged by John's description of this Joseph—comforted because disciples of Jesus can be afraid, and challenged because I don't want the same title given to me: "Kat, the disciple who feared ___________." Thank God he lets us trust him afraid.

8. **What do you learn about the Garden of the Crucifixion from John 19:41?**

What comes next in the story is action-packed. People are running, weeping, grasping, and then running again.

9. What prompted Mary to recognize Jesus not as the gardener but as the Lord? How does this moment resonate with you?

10. Based on John 20:18, what did Mary do with Jesus' command to go and preach the first Easter message? How does this encourage you or challenge you?

This scene moves me to my core. I've been studying Mary Magdalene ever since I wrote my first book, *No More Holding Back*, and I'm not over her. I'll never get over her. Mary Magdalene is an exemplary disciple of Jesus, and we are going to talk more about her in the next part of the lesson.

11. What unanswered questions do you have about the Gardens of the Crucifixion and Resurrection or anything else you've read so far?

12. What encouraged you most in your reading?

PART 3

UNDERSTANDING

Now that we've finished a close reading of the Scriptures, we're going to spend some time on interpretation: doing our best to understand what God was saying to the original audience and what he's teaching us through the process. But to do so, we need to learn his ways and consider how God's Word would have been understood by the original audience before applying the same truths to our own lives. "Scripture interpretation" may sound a little stuffy, but understanding what God means to communicate to us in the Bible is crucial to enjoying a close relationship with Jesus. Part 3 will enable you to answer the question *What does it mean?*

1. **Reread John 20:1–18. Underline anything that reminds you of Eden.**

20 Early on the first day of the week, while it was still dark, Mary
Magdalene came to the tomb and saw that the stone had been removed
from the tomb. 2 So she ran and went to Simon Peter and the other
disciple, the one whom Jesus loved, and said to them, "They have taken
the Lord out of the tomb, and we do not know where they have laid him."
3 Then Peter and the other disciple set out and went toward the tomb.
4 The two were running together, but the other disciple outran Peter
and reached the tomb first. 5 He bent down to look in and saw the linen
wrappings lying there, but he did not go in. 6 Then Simon Peter came,

following him, and went into the tomb. He saw the linen wrappings lying
there, [7] and the cloth that had been on Jesus' head, not lying with the
linen wrappings but rolled up in a place by itself. [8] Then the other disciple,
who reached the tomb first, also went in, and he saw and believed; [9] for
as yet they did not understand the scripture, that he must rise from the
dead. [10] Then the disciples returned to their homes.

[11] But Mary stood weeping outside the tomb. As she wept, she bent
over to look into the tomb; [12] and she saw two angels in white, sitting
where the body of Jesus had been lying, one at the head and the other
at the feet. [13] They said to her, "Woman, why are you weeping?" She said
to them, "They have taken away my Lord, and I do not know where they
have laid him." [14] When she had said this, she turned around and saw
Jesus standing there, but she did not know that it was Jesus. [15] Jesus
said to her, "Woman, why are you weeping? Whom are you looking
for?" Supposing him to be the gardener, she said to him, "Sir, if you
have carried him away, tell me where you have laid him, and I will take
him away." [16] Jesus said to her, "Mary!" She turned and said to him in
Hebrew, "Rabbouni!" (which means Teacher). [17] Jesus said to her, "Do
not hold on to me, because I have not yet ascended to the Father. But
go to my brothers and say to them, 'I am ascending to my Father and
your Father, to my God and your God.'" [18] Mary Magdalene went and
announced to the disciples, "I have seen the Lord"; and she told them
that he had said these things to her.

JOHN 20:1-18

2. **What would Jesus' resurrection mean for these groups of people?**

- **Romans:**

- **Jews:**

- **Disciples:**

3. **How does Jesus' resurrection impact your own life? In what ways could you use an epic redo in your personal life?**

4. **Write out a prayer asking God for what you need.**

MAKING CONNECTIONS

An important part of understanding the meaning of a Bible passage is getting a sense of its place in the broader storyline of Scripture. When we make connections between different parts of the Bible, we get a glimpse of the unity and cohesion of the Scriptures.

The Resurrection Garden needs no second act or understudies. Jesus alone is the culmination of God's redemptive commitment to his people. Jesus' resurrection is the focus, the pinnacle of John's Gospel and the inauguration of God's Kingdom here on earth. But there in the Resurrection Garden, Jesus was not alone. Mary Magdalene was in the garden too.

Women in gardens have been fooled, vilified, and degraded. They have turned everywhere but God, and the relational breakdown between men and women has shown up as a result. In Jesus' first conversation after the Resurrection, we see God drawing us back to what he always wanted: for women to hear his voice, hear him calling their names, and go tell their brothers, their fellow image bearers, their counterparts, the *true* news about God.

Men and women, we might mobilize and catalyze a generation of modern female disciples if we remind them that second in this passage to the all-important message that Jesus is risen from the dead is that the messenger of this news was a woman. Mary Magdalene was the first evangelist. The first person sent with the Good News of Jesus' resurrection. Or, put another way, she was the first to *bring it*.

Even more striking is the intentional parallel John draws between Mary Magdalene and Eve. The sacred echo here is that we have another woman in another garden but this time she listens to the right voice—the voice of God, who walks through the garden and announces that death is defeated, the serpent is crushed, paradise can be found. Look with me at the connections between the two women in their garden experiences.

EVE'S AND MARY MAGDALENE'S GARDEN EXPERIENCES

Eve (Genesis 1–3)	Mary Magdalene (John 20)
In the Garden of Eden, Eve was placed inside the garden by God's initiative.	In the Garden of Resurrection, Mary came from outside the garden by her own initiative.
We may be able to assume it was during the day that Eve was placed in the Garden of Eden because the lights had already been turned on (Genesis 1:14).	In Mary's story, it was still dark outside when she came to the Garden of Resurrection (John 20:1).
In the Garden of Eden, Eve was created *after* Adam.	In the Garden of Resurrection, Mary was the *first* person to see the resurrected Jesus—before Peter, before John.
In the Garden of Eden, Eve faced the fruit-producing Tree of Life.	In the Garden of Resurrection, Mary Magdalene faced a tomb of death.
Eve initiated death for all with her rebellion.	Mary Magdalene witnessed Jesus initiating resurrection life for all with his faithfulness.
In the Garden of Eden, the fruit Eve ate was available when she reached for it.	In the Garden of Resurrection, there was no body when Mary Magdalene looked in the grave.
Eve saw that the fruit from the Tree of the Knowledge of Good and Evil was good for food.	Mary Magdalene saw the risen Lord.
In the Garden of Eden, the serpent approached Eve with cunning questions that sowed doubt.	In the Garden of Resurrection, angels greeted Mary Magdalene, and then Jesus himself appeared, all of whom asked compassionate questions that sowed hope.
In the Garden of Eden, Eve hid her naked shame from God's presence before being ousted from Eden.	In the Garden of Resurrection, Mary wept without shame in Jesus' presence, and it was Jesus' burial clothes that were missing from his body.
Eve was deceived because she listened to the serpent's voice instead of trusting God's boundaries.	Mary was commissioned as she listened to Jesus' voice and trusted God's commands.
Eve rebelled.	Mary obeyed.

5. **What stands out to you in the side-by-side comparison of Eve's and Mary Magdalene's experiences in their gardens?**

6. **If you were to describe to a friend the meaning of this garden reversal, what would you say?**

The word the "gardener" speaks changes Mary's world forever. The risen Jesus calls Mary by name, and when she hears her name spoken in his voice, she turns around again. But this time she sees Jesus, her teacher, not the gardener (20:16). Once again the intimate and the cosmic conjoin: through the intimacy of Mary's name, the reality of the resurrection is revealed.

When Mary hears the voice of the risen Jesus, she sees the garden and the gardener differently. She no longer understands the empty tomb as a manifestation of death, but as testimony to the power and possibilities of life.[2]

Gail R. O'Day, "Gospel of John," in *Women's Bible Commentary*

Far too often men and women envision their enemy wagging a finger at them and saying something like "You are just like your mother, Eve." The Garden of Resurrection invites us instead to meditate on Jesus' message to Mary Magdalene: *Go and tell my brothers.* We don't have to be people who listen to lies, who disbelieve God, who walk in exile in a dry and broken land. By the power of the Holy Spirit, we can be children of the King, commissioned and free, running with the gospel news: Jesus is risen!

✿ ✿ ✿

Let's check back in on our Gardens Storyline.

THE GARDENS STORYLINE OF SCRIPTURE

Location	Scripture(s)	The Presence of God
The Garden of Eden	Genesis 1–3	God walked with Adam and Eve in the Garden of Eden.
The Garden of Ahasuerus	Esther 1, 7	God was working behind the scenes to save his people.
The Garden of Gethsemane	Matthew 26	Christ agonized over his impending crucifixion.
The Gardens of the Crucifixion and Resurrection	John 19–20	Christ appeared to Mary Magdalene and commissioned her to tell the other disciples of his resurrection.
The Garden City	Revelation 21–22	God will come to dwell with his people.

The Protection of God	The Provision of God	The Produce of God
God did not let Adam and Eve live forever in a fallen world.	God provided substitutionary atonement.	God planted the Tree of Life.
God did not let Haman's plan come to fruition.	God gave Esther and Mordecai courage.	God planted Esther in the Garden of Ahasuerus so she could ask the king to save the Jewish people.
God does not require us to die as a consequence of our sin, because Jesus willingly gave his life to save ours.	Christ gave Christians his life.	Jesus is the Vine, and we are the branches.
Christ paid the penalty for our sins on the cross.	Christ rose from the dead, securing our future resurrection.	Jesus' resurrection foreshadows the resurrection of all believers in Christ.
God will wipe away all the tears from our eyes.	God will make all things new.	God will plant a new Garden City.

1. **What about the Gardens of the Crucifixion and Resurrection resonates with you most? What part of the story piques your curiosity?**

2. **What did you learn about God in this lesson? And what did you learn about yourself in this lesson?**

3. **How should these truths shape your faith community and change you?**

PART 4

RESPONDING

The purpose of Bible study is to help you become more Christlike; that's why part 4 will include journaling space for your reflection on and responses to the content and a blank checklist for actionable next steps. You'll be able to process what you're learning so that you can live out the concepts and pursue Christlikeness. Part 4 will enable you to answer the questions *What truths is this passage teaching?* and *How do I apply this to my life?*

TODAY IS THE MONDAY AFTER EASTER. Evidence of the holiday is still there—I keep finding Easter-egg confetti in my hair, and I ate deviled eggs and lemon pie for breakfast.

On Mondays, my buddy Chris and I huddle for work; this week, post-Easter, we talk about the ways we took time to celebrate Christ's resurrection. My weekend was full of Easter-egg hunts and all things pastor's-wife life. I loved every minute. Chris, on the other hand, celebrated Easter by attaching a dying orchid to an oak tree in his backyard; he's a consummate gardener.

Chris had to explain to my nongardening self his efforts to jury-rig a dying flower onto a thriving tree. "That's how they live in the wild," he told me. Texas weather won't do the orchid any favors, but if his dying plant was going to have a chance, he needed to remove it from the pot, replant it in the crevices of a tall tree, and let the tree share its nutrients. Chris sent me pictures of his relocated orchid, and I must admit, it looked quite strange: the dark bark of the oak tree as the backdrop to a droopy, half-dead orchid and the moss propping up pitiful-looking petals.[3] It looked out of place. It looked like a lost cause.

I wonder how many of us picture our own lives and think things are out of place; how many of us feel like we are a lost cause. Or maybe it is not our lives that seem beyond help but the circumstances our loved ones endure. Your only hope, their only hope, is someone replanting us in places where we can grow.

To everyone feeling defeated, these truths are for you.

1. JESUS IS THE COSMIC GARDENER.

Some aspects of my life have been in a holding pattern for years, and I've done all the things I'm supposed to: the praying, the waiting, the counseling, the confessing, the reframing, the forgiveness. I've witnessed the holy work of God in me and through the circumstances. And my faith has increased. But honest to goodness, I need something more. Yes, the holy work of obedience and growing in Christlikeness will lead to a flourishing life this side of heaven. But this is not as good as it gets. Jesus is not done with us yet. He is not done with us until he replants us in the garden of the new heaven and new earth. Jesus conquered death in the Gardens of the Crucifixion and Resurrection so that we would make it through and be raised to life too.

I don't know what stories you've heard about Jesus in the past, but this is the real *real.* Jesus is the cosmic Gardener whose single-minded mission is to keep you connected to your life source, God. Maybe you're as lifeless as my friend Chris's orchid. Know this: Jesus is an even better gardener than Chris. He can replant you. Let him do his work. Open yourself up to trusting God, and let him tenderly nurse you back to spiritual health.

2. BEING FAITHFUL IN YOUR GARDEN IS POSSIBLE.

Maybe, like me, you can relate to the male disciples' failures in obedience. I sometimes find myself feeling far more like the yawning, sleepy disciples in the garden than Mary Magdalene, believing Jesus' words and sprinting off with the Good News. I can relate to the disciples who couldn't bear to watch Christ crucified and instead huddled afraid in the Upper Room. I've been absent when the people I love, the people who love me, have needed me most.

And then there's Mary Magdalene. Singled out as a shining example of true discipleship. Last at the cross, first at the tomb, and taking up sacred space in the Upper Room, she brought the message of Christ's resurrection to the other disciples. She shows us that being faithful in the gardens of our own lives is possible. Because Jesus rose from the dead, we don't have to obsess over the past, be anxious about the present, or fear the future. Whatever cycle you're worried about continuing, Jesus can break it! By the power of the Holy Spirit, faithfulness can define us as Christ's disciples. Let's let it!

Use this journaling space to process what you are learning.

Ask yourself how these truths impact your relationship with God and with others.

What is the Holy Spirit bringing to your mind as actionable next steps in your faith journey?

-
-
-

LESSON FIVE

TRUSTING GOD'S PLAN

THE GARDEN CITY:
THE FINAL GARDEN

SCRIPTURE: REVELATION 21–22

PART 1

CONTEXT

Before you begin your study, we will start with the context of the story we are about to read together: the setting, both cultural and historical; the people involved; and where our passage fits in the larger setting of Scripture. All these things help us make sense of what we're reading. Understanding the context of a Bible story is fundamental to reading Scripture well. Getting your bearings before you read will enable you to answer the question *What am I about to read?*

NO BIBLE-GARDEN FOOLISHNESS can keep us from our future resurrection. Because as sure as Jesus lived, died, and rose again, he is coming back to make all things new, including a garden. No matter what we encounter in the gardens of life, or what distrust and brokenness threads through our lives, our future is rooted in trust after doubt and life after death.

The garden stories of the Bible create all sorts of tension in us: between good and evil, life and death, exile and relationship. But the final garden in the Bible, where King Jesus comes back to walk among the trees with us forever, resolves every tension. God's original longing—for us to live in trust and relationship with him in the garden—will be fulfilled. Until then, we are waiting in hope. And yes, we're human—our hopeful waiting is not without trials or doubts. But we've got a vision of our future, thanks to John's final letter: the book of Revelation.

Revelation often intimidates Bible readers with its confusing symbols and strong language. The book is simultaneously a letter, an apocalyptic vision, and a prophetic book, which compounds and layers the meaning of the text. We're not going to dissect how to interpret the book—whether it describes past events, future events, or idealized events. We won't attempt to date Christ's future return to earth (and if you subscribe to someone's teaching that includes a countdown to the end of the world, may I gently suggest that you set all that aside?). If we get caught up in theories, we might miss the point of the whole book: that we can be faithful to God as we wait for his return.

This lesson is about the final garden in the Bible, which is actually a Garden City. John mixes his metaphors with countless Old and New Testament allusions and references, so the final Garden City is also the new Eden, new Temple, new Jerusalem, new creation, new paradise, and new garden. All God's redemptive activity throughout history finds its culmination in the last two chapters of the Bible, where God comes home to dwell with his people in a new paradise. The echoes of Eden are so loud in the text that you can barely hear John's vision of the future over Moses' and the prophets' writings.

Here's what we know for sure: However and whenever God chooses to make all things new, there will not be cherubim blocking us from his garden presence. There will be no serpents tempting us to rebel against God, no broken relationships, no tears over betrayal, and no death.

What you're about to read is the end of your story and mine. It is a story about God creating—not at the beginning but at the end. It's a story about God wiping away our tears. And we have so many, don't we?

What I hope you'll see is that the unconditionally loving God of Eden is back. He has been calling out for his people in every garden, and he is here to stay forever. Nothing and no one can mess with this garden. Praise God.

If you're walking into this lesson with destabilized faith, the Garden City is for you. Maybe you've felt as though doubt has barreled into your faith and almost taken you out at the knees but you're trying to get your footing once again. There is still reason to hope in God. None of your disappointments can take God away from you. He's here to stay.

And for those of us who hold in tension a desire to wait in hope while dealing with less-than-hopeful circumstances, the Garden City is for us, too. The cosmic Gardener is back to tend his creation; he's coming back to rescue us and replant us in one last garden.

1. **PERSONAL CONTEXT: What is going on in your life right now that might impact how you understand the story of the new Garden City? What do you hope to learn from this lesson?**

2. **SPIRITUAL CONTEXT: If you've never studied the Garden City before, what piques your curiosity? If you've studied this place or the book of Revelation before, what impressions and insights do you recall?**

3. **BIBLICAL CONTEXT: What questions come to mind as you read about the context of the new heaven and new earth or the book of Revelation? What questions do you wish you could have answered before studying this part of Scripture?**

PART 2

SEEING

Seeing the text is vital if we want the heart of the Scripture passage to sink in. We read slowly and intentionally through the text with the context in mind. As we practice close, thoughtful reading of Scripture, we pick up on phrases, implications, and meanings we might otherwise have missed. Part 2 includes close Scripture reading and observation questions to empower you to answer the question *What is the story saying?*

1. **Read Revelation 21–22. Underline anything that reminds you of any of the other gardens we've studied: the Garden of Eden, the Garden of Ahasuerus, the Garden of Gethsemane, or the Gardens of the Crucifixion and Resurrection.**

21 Then I saw a new heaven and a new earth; for the first heaven and
the first earth had passed away, and the sea was no more. [2] And I saw
the holy city, the new Jerusalem, coming down out of heaven from God,
prepared as a bride adorned for her husband. [3] And I heard a loud voice
from the throne saying,

"See, the home of God is among mortals.
He will dwell with them as their God;
they will be his peoples,
and God himself will be with them;

[4] he will wipe every tear from their eyes.
Death will be no more;
mourning and crying and pain will be no more,
for the first things have passed away."

[5] And the one who was seated on the throne said, "See, I am making
all things new." Also he said, "Write this, for these words are trustworthy
and true." [6] Then he said to me, "It is done! I am the Alpha and the Omega,
the beginning and the end. To the thirsty I will give water as a gift from
the spring of the water of life. [7] Those who conquer will inherit these
things, and I will be their God and they will be my children. [8] But as for the
cowardly, the faithless, the polluted, the murderers, the fornicators, the
sorcerers, the idolaters, and all liars, their place will be in the lake that
burns with fire and sulfur, which is the second death."

[9] Then one of the seven angels who had the seven bowls full of the
seven last plagues came and said to me, "Come, I will show you the bride,
the wife of the Lamb." [10] And in the spirit he carried me away to a great,
high mountain and showed me the holy city Jerusalem coming down
out of heaven from God. [11] It has the glory of God and a radiance like a
very rare jewel, like jasper, clear as crystal. [12] It has a great, high wall
with twelve gates, and at the gates twelve angels, and on the gates are
inscribed the names of the twelve tribes of the Israelites; [13] on the east
three gates, on the north three gates, on the south three gates, and on
the west three gates. [14] And the wall of the city has twelve foundations,
and on them are the twelve names of the twelve apostles of the Lamb.

[15] The angel who talked to me had a measuring rod of gold to measure
the city and its gates and walls. [16] The city lies foursquare, its length the
same as its width; and he measured the city with his rod, fifteen hundred
miles; its length and width and height are equal. [17] He also measured its
wall, one hundred forty-four cubits by human measurement, which the
angel was using. [18] The wall is built of jasper, while the city is pure gold,
clear as glass. [19] The foundations of the wall of the city are adorned with

every jewel; the first was jasper, the second sapphire, the third agate,
the fourth emerald, [20] the fifth onyx, the sixth carnelian, the seventh
chrysolite, the eighth beryl, the ninth topaz, the tenth chrysoprase, the
eleventh jacinth, the twelfth amethyst. [21] And the twelve gates are twelve
pearls, each of the gates is a single pearl, and the street of the city is pure
gold, transparent as glass.

[22] I saw no temple in the city, for its temple is the Lord God the
Almighty and the Lamb. [23] And the city has no need of sun or moon to
shine on it, for the glory of God is its light, and its lamp is the Lamb. [24] The
nations will walk by its light, and the kings of the earth will bring their glory
into it. [25] Its gates will never be shut by day—and there will be no night
there. [26] People will bring into it the glory and the honor of the nations.
[27] But nothing unclean will enter it, nor anyone who practices abomination
or falsehood, but only those who are written in the Lamb's book of life.

22 Then the angel showed me the river of the water of life, bright
as crystal, flowing from the throne of God and of the Lamb [2] through the
middle of the street of the city. On either side of the river is the tree of
life with its twelve kinds of fruit, producing its fruit each month; and the
leaves of the tree are for the healing of the nations. [3] Nothing accursed
will be found there any more. But the throne of God and of the Lamb will
be in it, and his servants will worship him; [4] they will see his face, and his
name will be on their foreheads. [5] And there will be no more night; they
need no light of lamp or sun, for the Lord God will be their light, and they
will reign forever and ever.

[6] And he said to me, "These words are trustworthy and true, for the
Lord, the God of the spirits of the prophets, has sent his angel to show his
servants what must soon take place."

[7] "See, I am coming soon! Blessed is the one who keeps the words of
the prophecy of this book."

[8] I, John, am the one who heard and saw these things. And when I
heard and saw them, I fell down to worship at the feet of the angel who

showed them to me; [9] but he said to me, "You must not do that! I am a
fellow servant with you and your comrades the prophets, and with those
who keep the words of this book. Worship God!"

[10] And he said to me, "Do not seal up the words of the prophecy of this
book, for the time is near. [11] Let the evildoer still do evil, and the filthy still
be filthy, and the righteous still do right, and the holy still be holy."

[12] "See, I am coming soon; my reward is with me, to repay according to
everyone's work. [13] I am the Alpha and the Omega, the first and the last,
the beginning and the end."

[14] Blessed are those who wash their robes, so that they will have the
right to the tree of life and may enter the city by the gates. [15] Outside are
the dogs and sorcerers and fornicators and murderers and idolaters, and
everyone who loves and practices falsehood.

[16] "It is I, Jesus, who sent my angel to you with this testimony for the
churches. I am the root and the descendant of David, the bright morning
star."

[17] The Spirit and the bride say, "Come."
And let everyone who hears say, "Come."
And let everyone who is thirsty come.
Let anyone who wishes take the water of life as a gift.

[18] I warn everyone who hears the words of the prophecy of this book: if
anyone adds to them, God will add to that person the plagues described
in this book; [19] if anyone takes away from the words of the book of this
prophecy, God will take away that person's share in the tree of life and in
the holy city, which are described in this book.

[20] The one who testifies to these things says, "Surely I am coming soon."
Amen. Come, Lord Jesus!

[21] The grace of the Lord Jesus be with all the saints. Amen.

REVELATION 21–22

2. **What stood out to you most in the Scripture reading?**

Revelation 21 and 22 are my two favorite chapters of the Bible. I've read them several times before, but I'd never noticed Revelation 22:3: that nothing accursed will be found in the new Garden City. My soul was filled with unspeakable joy as I imagined the serpent—and all that the serpent represents—gone, banished, no more.

3. **Write out what God says from his throne during the new-creation process in Revelation 21:3-4. Below the verses, summarize God's statements into one sentence or phrase. What is God saying? What does he mean?**

4. **Fill in the blanks using the verse prompts to complete the sentences.**

   God will create the new Garden City, and it will be like a cosmic wedding ceremony uniting heaven and earth. God will plant his Garden City on top of a great, high __________ (Revelation 21:10), and it will be like a fenced, square garden/Tabernacle/Temple, but this new Garden City won't need sunlight to grow its produce because it will be illuminated by the _______ ____ _______ and ____ _______ (Revelation 21:23). In the center of the garden will be the Tree of ________ (Revelation 22:2), and everyone will enjoy the fruit and healing it brings to the garden because the curse on the ground will be done away with. We will all cultivate the garden and ___________ God (Revelation 22:3, 9). With God, we will ________ together forever and ever (Revelation 22:5), just as he always envisioned.

5. **What unanswered questions do you have about the Garden City or anything else you've read so far?**

6. **What encouraged you most in your reading?**

PART 3

UNDERSTANDING

Now that we've finished a close reading of the Scriptures, we're going to spend some time on interpretation: doing our best to understand what God was saying to the original audience and what he's teaching us through the process. But to do so, we need to learn his ways and consider how God's Word would have been understood by the original audience before applying the same truths to our own lives. "Scripture interpretation" may sound a little stuffy, but understanding what God means to communicate to us in the Bible is crucial to enjoying a close relationship with Jesus. Part 3 will enable you to answer the question *What does it mean?*

JOHN WAS WRITING the book of Revelation to a group of Christians suffering under the Roman Empire 's oppression. These believers would have found his prophecies encouraging, especially because they felt powerless and hopeless at the time. I suspect a lot of us can relate.

1. **How do you imagine the Christians of the first century interpreted John's prophetic visions? And what about the final garden would be an encouragement to them?**

2. What about you? Do you feel hopeless or powerless about something in your own life? How do the last two chapters of the Bible encourage you?

Personally, I'm struggling with feeling trapped by my circumstances. I could tell you all the right things I believe about my theology. God is on his throne. God has good things planned for me. God planted me here. I can grow where I am planted. As long as I am here, God is with me.

But I'm also worried. Worried things will never change. Worried I'll have to give up some dreams. Worried I'll always feel this way: helpless.

So what is God's final intent for humanity? As is obvious from tracing the iconography of Eden through redemptive history, God's original intent *is* his final intent. Eden was the perfect plan, and God has never had any other. His goal was that the people of God might dwell in the place of God, enjoying the presence of God. This is all our heavenly Father has ever wanted for us. And everything that lies between Eden's gate and the New Jerusalem, the bulk of our Bibles, is in essence a huge rescue plan. In fact, we could summarize the plot line of the Bible into one cosmic question: "How do we get *'Ādām* back into the garden?" In Genesis 3 humanity was driven out; in Revelation 21–22 they are welcomed home.[1]

Sandra L. Richter, *The Epic of Eden*

That's why reading about the final garden in the Bible brings me so much joy. Things will change eventually. The dreams lost or delayed will be realized eventually. And help is on its way. God is not just coming back to set things right; he is also coming to make all things new—and then he's going to invite you and me to join him in the newness.

3. What is the one thing you most look forward to never crying over again? Name it below. Will that thing be in the new Garden City?

My father's death by suicide ranks at the top of my list. I've shed so many tears over the end of his life that I've become dehydrated. What I find most comforting about the final garden is that God will be close enough to us to reach out and wipe our tears. Whether that means a physical hand gently absorbing our tears or a spiritual reality where tears don't have a place anymore, our grief will die with death. The wounds we carry will get left outside the garden gates.

4. Take a moment to write out a message to the Lord thanking him for your future reality. Ask him for what you need in this moment.

MAKING CONNECTIONS

An important part of understanding the meaning of a Bible passage is getting a sense of its place in the broader storyline of Scripture. When we make connections between different parts of the Bible, we get a glimpse of the unity and cohesion of the Scriptures.

One of the nerdiest books I own happens to be one of my favorites: *Commentary on the New Testament Use of the Old Testament.* I love all the connections the authors make between the Old Testament and the New Testament. Implicit in the title is the fact that God's Word is a unified story that points to Jesus, that all Scripture is related. But for me, this reference book is also a reminder that God is working—in and through our lives—toward a certain outcome. If God can write a cohesive story over fifteen hundred years through over forty authors and create sixty-six Bible books that all lead us to Jesus, certainly he can order my steps and yours. Our lives are not left up to chance. Everything we are going through has a purpose.

> The last vision of Revelation is a magnificent view of the new creation, which is, we will argue, portrayed as equivalent to the new Jerusalem, the eschatological cubic temple, and to end-time Eden, the eternal home of God's people.[2]
>
> **G. K. Beale and Sean M. McDonough, "Revelation," in *Commentary on the New Testament Use of the Old Testament***

Your life has meaning, and everything you're experiencing is part of God's bigger redemption story. His plan won't fail. God won't fail you. The future reality we are praying for is real. Our God, the cosmic Gardener, has worked through and will continue to work through our metaphorical life gardens and will eventually replant us in the new and final garden with him. Culmination is coming. Renewal is in your future. Renovation and restoration are guaranteed.

God opens and closes the story of redemption with creation scenes that involve celestial gardens. Let's zero in on only a handful of the hundreds of connections between these gardens made in the *Commentary on the New Testament Use of the Old Testament.*

HOW THE GARDEN CITY (REVELATION 21:1-5) FULFILLS OLD TESTAMENT PROPHECIES[3]

New Testament Scripture about the Garden City	Corresponding Old Testament Prophecies
REVELATION 21:1: "Then I saw a new heaven and a new earth; for the first heaven and the first earth had passed away, and the sea was no more."	**ISAIAH 65:17:** "I am about to create new heavens and a new earth; the former things shall not be remembered or come to mind." **ISAIAH 66:22:** "As the new heavens and the new earth, which I will make, shall remain before me, says the LORD; so shall your descendants and your name remain."
REVELATION 21:2: "I saw the holy city, the new Jerusalem, coming down out of heaven from God, prepared as a bride adorned for her husband."	**ISAIAH 52:1:** "Awake, awake, put on your strength, O Zion! Put on your beautiful garments, O Jerusalem, the holy city; for the uncircumcised and the unclean shall enter you no more." **ISAIAH 61:10:** "I will greatly rejoice in the LORD, my whole being shall exult in my God; for he has clothed me with the garments of salvation, he has covered me with the robe of righteousness, as a bridegroom decks himself with a garland, and as a bride adorns herself with her jewels."
REVELATION 21:3: "I heard a loud voice from the throne saying, 'See, the home of God is among mortals. He will dwell with them as their God; they will be his peoples, and God himself will be with them.'"	**EZEKIEL 37:26-28:** "I will make a covenant of peace with them; it shall be an everlasting covenant with them; and I will bless them and multiply them, and will set my sanctuary among them forevermore. My dwelling place shall be with them; and I will be their God, and they shall be my people." **EZEKIEL 43:7:** "[The Lord] said to [Ezekiel]: Mortal, this is the place of my throne and the place for the soles of my feet, where I will reside among the people of Israel forever."

New Testament Scripture about the Garden City	Corresponding Old Testament Prophecies
REVELATION 21:4: "'He will wipe every tear from their eyes. Death will be no more; mourning and crying and pain will be no more, for the first things have passed away.'"	**ISAIAH 25:7-8:** "[The LORD of hosts] will swallow up death forever. Then the Lord GOD will wipe away the tears from all faces, and the disgrace of his people he will take away from all the earth, for the LORD has spoken." **ISAIAH 35:10:** "The ransomed of the LORD shall return, and come to Zion with singing; everlasting joy shall be upon their heads; they shall obtain joy and gladness, and sorrow and sighing shall flee away."
REVELATION 21:5: "The one who was seated on the throne said, 'See, I am making all things new.' Also he said, 'Write this, for these words are trustworthy and true.'"	**ISAIAH 43:18-19:** "Do not remember the former things, or consider the things of old. I am about to do a new thing; now it springs forth, do you not perceive it? I will make a way in the wilderness and rivers in the desert." **ISAIAH 65:17:** "I am about to create new heavens and a new earth; the former things shall not be remembered or come to mind." **ISAIAH 66:22:** "As the new heavens and the new earth, which I will make, shall remain before me, says the LORD; so shall your descendants and your name remain."

God is not deliberating what he's going to do with you. He's not weighing his options or wrestling with his next step. His mind is made up: He's going to redeem your story. You don't need to second-guess his intentions or question his motives or struggle with suspicion that he's holding out on you. He's not. Just as he's prophesied for generations, he is going to fulfill his promises to us. To you. To me. You can count on God. He is trustworthy. Everything you're going through is not a waste. God is working out his plan. God is seeing to it that you accomplish your purpose.

5. On a scale from 1 to 10, 1 being "not at all" and 10 being "completely," how much do you trust God with your future? How does your trust level show up in your life?

1 2 3 4 5 6 7 8 9 10

6. For the first-century Christians, who knew the Old Testament well, what do you think it would mean to them to see God fulfilling and repurposing so many Old Testament prophecies in Revelation 21 and 22?

[It's] implicitly suggested that [the temple's] purpose was to point to a future time when it would encompass the whole world (much like an architect's model of a newly planned building is but a small replica of what is to be built on a much larger scale). . . . This imagery ultimately appears to be traceable back to the garden of Eden itself.[4]

G. K. Beale and Sean M. McDonough, "Revelation," in *Commentary on the New Testament Use of the Old Testament*

✿ ✿ ✿

Let's check back in on our Gardens Storyline.

THE GARDENS STORYLINE OF SCRIPTURE

Location	Scripture(s)	The Presence of God
The Garden of Eden	Genesis 1–3	God walked with Adam and Eve in the Garden of Eden.
The Garden of Ahasuerus	Esther 1, 7	God was working behind the scenes to save his people.
The Garden of Gethsemane	Matthew 26	Christ agonized over his impending crucifixion.
The Gardens of the Crucifixion and Resurrection	John 19–20	Christ appeared to Mary Magdalene and commissioned her to tell the other disciples of his resurrection.
The Garden City	Revelation 21–22	God will come to dwell with his people.

The Protection of God	The Provision of God	The Produce of God
God did not let Adam and Eve live forever in a fallen world.	God provided substitutionary atonement.	God planted the Tree of Life.
God did not let Haman's plan come to fruition.	God gave Esther and Mordecai courage.	God planted Esther in the Garden of Ahasuerus so she could ask the king to save the Jewish people.
God does not require us to die as a consequence of our sin, because Jesus willingly gave his life to save ours.	Christ gave Christians his life.	Jesus is the Vine, and we are the branches.
Christ paid the penalty for our sins on the cross.	Christ rose from the dead, securing our future resurrection.	Jesus' resurrection foreshadows the resurrection of all believers in Christ.
God will wipe away all the tears from our eyes.	God will make all things new.	God will plant a new Garden City.

1. **What about the final garden story resonates with you most? What part of the story piques your curiosity?**

2. **What did you learn about God in this lesson? And what did you learn about yourself in this lesson?**

3. **How should these truths shape your faith community and change you?**

PART 4

RESPONDING

The purpose of Bible study is to help you become more Christlike; that's why part 4 will include journaling space for your reflection on and responses to the content and a blank checklist for actionable next steps. You'll be able to process what you're learning so that you can live out the concepts and pursue Christlikeness. Part 4 will enable you to answer the questions *What truths is this passage teaching?* and *How do I apply this to my life?*

LATELY I'VE BEEN WAKING UP in the middle of the night, feeling distraught about the future. Even though I know I'll look back on this season and wonder why I spent so many hours on and shed so many tears over something God was working hard to make right, I'm still human. While I waste my emotional bandwidth flowcharting all that could be hard and go wrong, my God, your God, is on his throne. His watchful, caring eye has not blinked once on our hardships. All along he's been by our side, shouldering our burdens, attentive to our every need.

While we worry, he's working. As we grieve, he's restoring. In the middle of our doubts, he's confidently securing our hopeful future. Although it may feel as though things will never change, they will. He's promised.

Here are the lessons God is trying to teach me through the final garden story. I am praying they encourage you, too.

1. THIS IS NOT THE END.

God is not finished. He is still bringing your story to completion. And until he is done, we need you here. I'm waiting on a twenty-year-old dream to come to fruition, and I'm so tired, so weary from waiting. I've prayed all the right prayers. I've sought all the godly wisdom. Twenty years later, not one of the aches in my heart has been wasted. In a way only God can do, he's kept me close to him and reminded me time and time again, *This is not the end.*

I'm not saying it's going to be easy. Trusting God is a spiritual battle, not a spiritual vacation. What I'm saying is that this is not the end. If you're staring down impossible circumstances, if your inner critic is screaming through a megaphone, *There's no way out!*—fix your eyes on Jesus. He will lead you through. God has spoken a message to you through every garden story in Scripture: *This is not the end.* Dead ends are just the beginning for God. Trust him through the hopelessness. Keep holding on.

2. GOD IS GOING TO MAKE ALL THINGS NEW.

I'd settle for *making all things better*, but that's not God's standard. He doesn't just make things better; he has the power to make things new, different. *New* has almost lost all meaning to me; every advertisement I come across is promoting some upgrade, some *new!*, to the product being promoted. But God isn't trying to sell us something. He wants to *give* us something: a new life.

If you are wishing for something better, desperate for something good to happen in your life, be encouraged. God is the only One in your life who has the power to create something from nothing. When God re-creates, he offers himself to us as a gift, a guarantee that this is not as good as it gets. He's coming back, and when he does, you'll have all the makings of a brand-new life. Until then, he's going to prove to you, in time, that he's not waiting to give you the good stuff. The newness has already started.

Use this journaling space to process what you are learning.

Ask yourself how these truths impact your relationship with God and with others.

What is the Holy Spirit bringing to your mind as actionable next steps in your faith journey?

- ✿
- ✿
- ✿

As You Go

YOU DID IT. You studied five Bible stories where gardens point us to God's pursuing presence and help us see that trusting him leads to a life of abundant goodness.

- The Garden of Eden shows us how easy it is for us to trust ourselves, to listen to the wrong voices—but God's longing, his heart, his original plan has always been for us to walk with him in the cool of the evening, to bring him our questions and doubts and find flourishing life in relationships. You can trust God's boundaries.
- The Garden of Ahasuerus reveals that our sin creates division—not just between us and God but also between us and others. In this garden, the absence of flourishing points us to the path to abundance: where men and women call each other to better things, partnering together and trusting God. You can trust Christ's kingship.

- The Garden of Gethsemane brings us back to a God who walks in the garden, but this time he joins us in the garden that we have broken. He participates in our suffering. He feels the depths of our grief. This is not the garden we were made for, but God steps into it so that we can trust his presence even here. You can trust Christ's sacrifice.
- The Gardens of the Crucifixion and Resurrection change the game. Jesus is crucified and comes back to life in a garden so that we can return to a flourishing life with him. You can trust Christ's resurrection.
- The Garden City is our ultimate hope. Exile is not our future; abundance is. No matter what we face now, God has told us the ending: We will be with him in the garden forever. You can trust God's plan for your future.

I hope this study has transformed you the way it has transformed me. I'm closing this Bible study with newfound confidence in God's character, increased faith, and certainty that I can trust God with my questions, concerns, and circumstances.

PS: I've loved this journey with you, and I hope you join me again—this time, for the *Deserts* study.

THE GARDENS STORYLINE OF SCRIPTURE

Location	Scripture(s)	The Presence of God
The Garden of Eden	Genesis 1–3	God walked with Adam and Eve in the Garden of Eden.
The Garden of Ahasuerus	Esther 1, 7	God was working behind the scenes to save his people.
The Garden of Gethsemane	Matthew 26	Christ agonized over his impending crucifixion.
The Gardens of the Crucifixion and Resurrection	John 19–20	Christ appeared to Mary Magdalene and commissioned her to tell the other disciples of his resurrection.
The Garden City	Revelation 21–22	God will come to dwell with his people.

The Protection of God	The Provision of God	The Produce of God
God did not let Adam and Eve live forever in a fallen world.	God provided substitutionary atonement.	God planted the Tree of Life.
God did not let Haman's plan come to fruition.	God gave Esther and Mordecai courage.	God planted Esther in the Garden of Ahasuerus so she could ask the king to save the Jewish people.
God does not require us to die as a consequence of our sin, because Jesus willingly gave his life to save ours.	Christ gave Christians his life.	Jesus is the Vine, and we are the branches.
Christ paid the penalty for our sins on the cross.	Christ rose from the dead, securing our future resurrection.	Jesus' resurrection foreshadows the resurrection of all believers in Christ.
God will wipe away all the tears from our eyes.	God will make all things new.	God will plant a new Garden City.

Each **Storyline Bible Study** is five lessons long and can be paired with its thematic partner for a seamless ten-week study. Complement the *Gardens* study with

DESERTS

JOURNEYING THROUGH THE WILDERNESS TO EXPERIENCE GOD'S PROVISION

The *Deserts* Bible study will help you discover an all-important truth: God meets your needs in your metaphorical deserts. Like he has done with everyone else he's led through the desert, he will accompany you faithfully to the other side of this part of your journey.

LESSON ONE: Going through Rejection to Get to Protection
The Deserts of Shur and Beersheba: Where Hagar Meets and Names God
GENESIS 16, 21

LESSON TWO: Going through Resentment to Get to Forgiveness
The Desert of Dothan: Where Joseph Gets Thrown into a Pit
GENESIS 37, 45, 50

LESSON THREE: Going through Insecurity to Get to Belonging
The Desert of Sinai: Where Moses and the Israelites Wander in the Wilderness
NUMBERS 11, 14

LESSON FOUR: Going through Trials to Get to Ministry
The Desert of Judea: Where Jesus Is Tested
MATTHEW 3–4

LESSON FIVE: Going through Scarcity to Get to Abundance
The Deserts of Ministry: Where Jesus Feeds the Multitudes
MATTHEW 14, 15

Acknowledgments

WITHOUT MY FAMILY'S SUPPORT, the **Storyline Bible Studies** would just be a dream. I'm exceedingly grateful for a family that prays and cheers for me when I step out to try something new. To my husband, Aaron; son, Caleb; and mom, Noemi: You three sacrificed the most to ensure that I had enough time and space to write. Thank you. And to all my extended family: I know an army of Armstrongs was praying and my family in Austin was cheering me on to the finish line. Thank you.

NavPress and Tyndale teams: Thank you for believing in me. You wholeheartedly embraced the concept, and you've made this project better in every way possible. Special thanks to David Zimmerman, my amazing editor Caitlyn Carlson, Elizabeth Schroll, Olivia Eldredge, David Geeslin, and the entire editorial and marketing teams.

All my friends rallied to pray for this project when I was stressed about the deadlines. Thank you. We did it! Without your intercession, these wouldn't be complete. I want to give special thanks to my closest friends and my Tuesday night Bible-study group: Ashley W. and G., Abby, Amy, Ellen, Hanah, Kylie, Laura L. and V., Lauren, Leigh, Lisa, Regina, Sami, Sarah, Sydney, and Tabitha.

Resources for Deeper Study

OLD TESTAMENT

The Africana Bible: Reading Israel's Scriptures from Africa and the African Diaspora, ed. Hugh R. Page Jr.

And God Spoke to Abraham: Preaching from the Old Testament by Fleming Rutledge

Bearing God's Name: Why Sinai Still Matters by Carmen Joy Imes

The Epic of Eden: A Christian Entry into the Old Testament by Sandra L. Richter

The IVP Bible Background Commentary: Old Testament by John H. Walton, Victor H. Matthews, and Mark W. Chavalas

The Lost World of Genesis One: Ancient Cosmology and the Origins Debate by John H. Walton

Opening Israel's Scriptures by Ellen F. Davis

The Pentateuch as Narrative: A Biblical-Theological Commentary, Library of Biblical Interpretation, by John H. Sailhamer

The Universal Story: Genesis 1–11, Transformative Word Series, by Dru Johnson

NEW TESTAMENT

Echoes of Scripture in the Gospels by Richard B. Hays

The Gospel according to Matthew, New Collegeville Bible Commentary, by Barbara E. Reid

The Gospels as Stories: A Narrative Approach to Matthew, Mark, Luke, and John by Jeannine K. Brown

An Introduction to the New Testament, 2nd ed., by D. A. Carson and Douglas J. Moo

The Jewish Annotated New Testament: New Revised Standard Version Bible Translation, 2nd ed., eds. Amy-Jill Levine and Marc Zvi Brettler

John: A Commentary, The New Testament Library, by Marianne Meye Thompson

John's Wisdom: A Commentary on the Fourth Gospel by Ben Witherington III

Matthew, The Two Horizons New Testament Commentary, by Jeannine K. Brown and Kyle Roberts

The New Testament in Its World: An Introduction to the History, Literature, and Theology of the First Christians by N. T. Wright and Michael F. Bird

True to Our Native Land: An African American New Testament Commentary, ed. Brian K. Blount

BIBLE STUDY

Commentary on the New Testament Use of the Old Testament, eds. G. K. Beale and D. A. Carson

Dictionary of Biblical Imagery, eds. Leland Ryken, James C. Wilhoit, and Tremper Longman III

The Drama of Scripture: Finding Our Place in the Biblical Story by Craig G. Bartholomew and Michael W. Goheen

From Beginning to Forever: A Study of the Grand Narrative of Scripture by Elizabeth Woodson

How (Not) to Read the Bible: Making Sense of the Anti-Women, Anti-Science, Pro-Violence, Pro-Slavery and Other Crazy-Sounding Parts of Scripture by Dan Kimball

How to Read the Bible as Literature . . . and Get More out of It by Leland Ryken

Literarily: How Understanding Bible Genres Transforms Bible Study by Kristie Anyabwile

The Mission of God: Unlocking the Bible's Grand Narrative by Christopher J. H. Wright

"Reading Scripture as a Coherent Story" by Richard Bauckham, in *The Art of Reading Scripture*, eds. Ellen F. Davis and Richard B. Hays

Reading While Black: African American Biblical Interpretation as an Exercise in Hope by Esau McCaulley

Read the Bible for a Change: Understanding and Responding to God's Word by Ray Lubeck

Scripture as Communication: Introducing Biblical Hermeneutics by Jeannine K. Brown

South Asia Bible Commentary: A One-Volume Commentary on the Whole Bible, ed. Brian Wintle

Theological Bible Commentary, eds. Gail R. O'Day and David L. Petersen

Vindicating the Vixens: Revisiting Sexualized, Vilified, and Marginalized Women of the Bible, ed. Sandra Glahn

What Is the Bible and How Do We Understand It? by Dennis R. Edwards

Women's Bible Commentary, 3rd ed., eds. Carol A. Newsom, Sharon H. Ringe, and Jacqueline E. Lapsley

Words of Delight: A Literary Introduction to the Bible by Leland Ryken

About the Author

KAT ARMSTRONG was born in Houston, Texas, where the humidity ruins her Mexi-German curls. She is a powerful voice in our generation as a sought-after Bible teacher, preacher, and leader, and she's on a mission to spark holy curiosity in a generation of Bible readers. She holds a master's degree from Dallas Theological Seminary and is pursuing a doctorate of ministry in New Testament context. Kat is the author of *No More Holding Back*, *The In-Between Place*, and the **Storyline Bible Studies**. She is the cofounder of the Polished Network and the host of the *Holy Curiosity* podcast. She and her husband, Aaron, have been married for over twenty years; live in McKinney, Texas, with their son, Caleb; and attend the church in McKinney where Aaron serves as the lead pastor.

KATARMSTRONG.COM
@KATARMSTRONG1

THESTORYLINEPROJECT.COM
@THESTORYLINEPROJECT

Notes

LESSON ONE | TRUSTING GOD'S BOUNDARIES

1. James Swanson, "עֵדֶן," in *Dictionary of Biblical Languages with Semantic Domains: Hebrew (Old Testament)* (Oak Harbor, WA: Logos Research Systems, 1997).
2. Rodney S. Sadler Jr., "Genesis," in *The Africana Bible: Reading Israel's Scriptures from Africa and the African Diaspora*, ed. Hugh R. Page Jr. (Minneapolis: Fortress Press, 2010), 70.
3. Glenn Kreider, "Eve: The Mother of All Seducers?" in *Vindicating the Vixens: Revisiting Sexualized, Vilified, and Marginalized Women of the Bible*, ed. Sandra Glahn (Grand Rapids: Kregel, 2017), 137.
4. Ellen F. Davis, *Opening Israel's Scriptures* (New York: Oxford University Press, 2019), 21.
5. For more on the Tabernacle and its connections to the Garden of Eden, see "What's So Special about the Tabernacle?," May 2, 2022, the BibleProject podcast, https://bibleproject.com/podcast/whats-so-special-about-tabernacle.

LESSON TWO | TRUSTING CHRIST'S KINGSHIP

1. Holly J. Carey, *Women Who Do: Female Disciples in the Gospels* (Grand Rapids: Eerdmans, 2023), 108–11.
2. If my friend Sharifa had not written an outstanding chapter about Queen Vashti in one of my favorite Bible commentaries, *Vindicating the Vixens*, I might have missed Queen Vashti's significance in the book of Esther. See Sharifa Stevens, "Vashti: Dishonored for Having Honor," in *Vindicating the Vixens: Revisiting Sexualized, Vilified, and Marginalized Women of the Bible*, ed. Sandra Glahn (Grand Rapids: Kregel, 2017).
3. Tremper Longman III and Raymond B. Dillard, *An Introduction to the Old Testament*, 2nd ed. (Grand Rapids: Zondervan Academic, 2006), 218.
4. Stevens, "Vashti," 242.

5. John H. Walton, Victor H. Matthews, and Mark W. Chavalas, *The IVP Bible Background Commentary: Old Testament* (Downers Grove, IL: InterVarsity Press, 2000), 484.
6. Walton et al., *IVP Bible Background Commentary*, 484.
7. Walton et al., *IVP Bible Background Commentary*, 484.
8. Stevens, "Vashti," 243.
9. Walton et al., *IVP Bible Background Commentary*, 485.
10. The parenthetical summaries in this list are headings in Esther 2–6 of the NRSV.

LESSON THREE | TRUSTING CHRIST'S SACRIFICE

1. Jeannine K. Brown and Kyle Roberts, *Matthew*, The Two Horizons New Testament Commentary (Grand Rapids: Eerdmans, 2018), 241.
2. Barbara E. Reid, *The Gospel according to Matthew*, New Collegeville Bible Commentary (Collegeville, MN: Liturgical Press, 2005), 132.
3. Colloquial name for Baylor University Medical Center.
4. Craig L. Blomberg, "Matthew," in *Commentary on the New Testament Use of the Old Testament*, ed. G. K. Beale and D. A. Carson (Grand Rapids: Baker Academic, 2007), 93. "As Jesus prays (26:38), the triple refrain of Ps. 42:5, 11; 43:5 appears to lie in the background."
5. Brian Wintle, "Matthew," in *South Asia Bible Commentary: A One-Volume Commentary on the Whole Bible*, ed. Brian Wintle (Grand Rapids: Zondervan, 2015), 1279.
6. U2, "Where the Streets Have No Name," track 1 on *The Joshua Tree*, Island Records, 1987.

LESSON FOUR | TRUSTING CHRIST'S RESURRECTION

1. "Because He Lives," by Bill and Gloria Gaither, track A1 on The Bill Gaither Trio, *Because He Lives*, Heart Warming Records, 1971.
2. Gail R. O'Day, "Gospel of John," in *Women's Bible Commentary*, 3rd ed., ed. Carol A. Newsom, Sharon H. Ringe, and Jacqueline E. Lapsley (Louisville: Westminster John Knox Press, 2012), 528.
3. Oak trees can vary in color; some have dark bark.

LESSON FIVE | TRUSTING GOD'S PLAN

1. Sandra L. Richter, *The Epic of Eden: A Christian Entry into the Old Testament* (Downers Grove, IL: InterVarsity Press, 2008), 129.
2. G. K. Beale and Sean M. McDonough, "Revelation," in *Commentary on the New Testament Use of the Old Testament*, ed. G. K. Beale and D. A. Carson (Grand Rapids: Baker Academic, 2007), 1150.
3. Beale and McDonough, "Revelation," 1150–51.
4. Beale and McDonough, "Revelation," 1155.